a little light on
Ascension

a little light on
Ascension

Diana Cooper

FINDHORN
Press

First published by Findhorn Press 1997
Reprinted many times

ISBN 1-899171-81-9

British Library Cataloguing-in-Publication Data.
A catalogue record for this book is available
from the British Library.

Set in Times by Findhorn Press
Cover design by Thierry Bogliolo
Cover illustration "Angelic Guide" © 2001 Emery Bear

Printed and bound by WS Bookwell, Finland

Published by
Findhorn Press
305a The Park, Findhorn
Forres IV36 3TE
Scotland, UK
tel 01309 690582
fax 01309 690036
email info@findhornpress.com
findhornpress.com

Contents

Introduction to Kumeka 9
1: Ascension 13
2: Meditation 18
3: Purification 22
4: Freedom 29
5: Inner Peace 33
6: Simplicity 36
7: Abundance 40
8: Manifestation 46
9: Discernment 50
10: Protection 55
11: Finding Your Mission 61
12: The Monad 66
13: Fourth–Dimensional Chakras 69
14: Light Levels 78
15: The Mahatma Energy 81
16: Reiki and Spiritual Healing 86
17: Wake-Up Calls 92
18: Deep Cleansing 99
19: Intergalactic Work 104
20: Petitioning for Release of Karma 108
21: Mantras 112
22: Spirit Guides 118
23: Angels 122
24: Archangels 127
25: Ascended Masters 133
26: Ascension Chambers 138
27: Decrees 142
28: The Antakarana 146
29: Ritual and Ceremony 150
30: Armageddon 154
31: Oneness 160
32: Codes and Keys 164
33: Keys to Ascension 169

I dedicate this book to Shaaron

and

Kumeka, Lord of Light, Ascended Master

with love and gratitude

Introduction to Kumeka

On 31 December, 1994, New Year's Eve, various friends were coming to my home to meditate and set goals for the coming year. One by one they dropped out until only Shaaron and I remained. I did not know Shaaron that well. She was more of a long-term acquaintance than a friend but I did know that she was becoming more and more psychic.

During the course of the evening Kumeka started to communicate with us. He told us he had been waiting until we were ready. He could not contact us directly when we were on our own but together our vibration was high enough for him to reach. Apparently for some time he had been impressing me with information when I was working with clients and writing and Shaaron when she was doing her tarot readings. I really can't remember a great deal about that evening and I did not write down what he told us. All I know is that it is the best New Year's Eve I have ever experienced and it changed my life.

I later learnt that Kumeka had first noticed my light twenty years before when I was living on an island off the coast of Venezuela. I was surprised, saying I did not think I had a light then but he said I did and that since then he had been waiting for me to be ready to receive his guidance. To do this he had brought Shaaron and myself together from opposite ends of the world when the time was right.

He said that it had to be Shaaron who worked with me because we are from the same Monad or Divine Spark, so we are spiritual cousins.

Since then both Shaaron and I have grown and developed. She has always been very psychic, with past lives as a very powerful shaman. She now sees and hears Kumeka so clearly that it is as if he is a real, solid person sitting in the room with us. For a long time she was very sceptical and dismissed all that was happening, including all the information he gave us for our own growth and that of others. Now she is more accepting but not particularly involved.

Kumeka said that Shaaron is much more psychically developed than I am. However, I am much more spiritually developed than she is. In order to spread light through me he had to bring us together as I could not make a connection to him on my own. For about a year Shaaron and I had to be together in order to link with Kumeka. Then he said this was no longer necessary and we could each access him independently. We still work together, however, if there is specific information I need from him.

Nowadays Kumeka often overshadows me, in other words, melds his consciousness with mine and speaks through me. When this happens I feel bigger and totally calm. Sometimes I get tired or frazzled and then I cannot maintain the vibration which allows him to enter and I feel myself slipping back to being the limited me.

Shaaron and I have gradually become aware that Kumeka is a much greater, mightier being than we had any concept of. So who is He, this amazing, incredible Being of Light who is one of our guides?

Kumeka has never been incarnated on Earth but has ascended from another planet. Until recently he has worked in two of the other twelve universes. Now he has started to connect with ours. We on Earth have been influenced by seven of the twelve rays available in the Cosmos. We are now opening up to the influence of a higher ray, the Eighth Ray. Kumeka is Chohan or Master of the Eighth Ray.

Earth has finally earned the right to have Lord Kumeka's attention and presence.

The Eighth Ray is that of higher cleansing. Kumeka is in charge of planetary cleansing, especially of power points in this and other planets. He oversees the purification of the light portals and ley lines. He works with the Archangels and Seraphim and is bringing the quality of joy to the planet. His ascension chamber — or light chamber — in the etheric is above Caracas, Venezuela.

Kumeka helps with the removal from humans of alien implants, elementals, negative entities and even unhelpful mindsets. When you invoke him for help, you can also call on Vywamus, Archangel Michael and Djwhal Khul. Together they make a mighty team.

He rarely offers esoteric information. I have to formulate a question and then he will respond if it is permitted that an answer be given. I only discovered an amazing piece of information when I asked him if Jesus Christ was indeed the only son of God. Kumeka replied that Jesus was the only son/daughter of God ever to have incarnated on Earth. He explained that a son/daughter of God is a being of God energy once diluted and that there are twelve sons/daughters of God working through the universes of which he, Lord Kumeka, is one. Avatars, such as Sai Baba and Mother Meera, are sons of sons of God, in other words, the God energy twice diluted.

He is Lord Kumeka, Lord of Light, Ascended Master and Chohan of the Eighth Ray. He is a son/daughter of God and has always had direct connection with his Father and the responsibility that goes with that.

Kumeka has worked in a different galaxy from ours. He tells us that there are several that we do not know about yet, which are not contained within the same time frame that we understand. These galaxies need to evolve too.

Because our planet is raising its vibratory rate, we are able to accommodate the new higher ray, thus earning the right for Kumeka to come here. He says that the nearer our planet gets to Ascension, the more beings like him will come to help.

As above so below. Although it is perfectly logical that the Highest of the High resonate with others on a like vibration, I was surprised to find that Ascended Masters have particular friends. Two of Kumeka's particular friends, who work in this universe, are White Eagle, whose wonderful teachings are known to many, and Merlin.

When clients come to me or to my workshops, Kumeka often continues to work with them and help them after the session.

It is almost beyond my comprehension that Kumeka could want to connect with me. I feel honoured, privileged and humble to work with him. This book contains his energy and will connect you to him.

Exercise — Visualisation to meet Lord Kumeka

1. Relax, become quiet and still.

2. Visualise yourself going up pure white steps to an enormous temple.

3. Push open the huge doors and enter the sacred space. It is empty except for Kumeka.

4. Go to the altar and light a candle.

5. Sit by Lord Kumeka. Introduce yourself and tell him what you want.

6. Ask any questions or for any help you need.

7. Thank him and leave.

1: ASCENSION

Ascension means raising our vibration to the level of Light. Because every thought, word, emotion and action is a vibration which creates our aura, Ascension entails purifying our thoughts, cleansing our emotions and choosing loving action for the highest good until we radiate at that higher level. Then we live in joy and freedom.

Those who live at a purely physical level of understanding, believing only what they can see, hear and feel, metaphorically chug through life in third gear. From above they appear to be clutching the steering wheel, terrified of what might happen to them. They live by human laws, cursing and blaming other drivers and are often scared to change lane for fear of the consequences. Frequently they believe their lane is the only lane anyone should be in.

As we become more open to spiritual matters and especially to unconditional love, we change into fourth gear, or the fourth dimension. This means driving through life in a more relaxed and trusting way, honouring all other drivers on their way and following our intuition. We know that each person's journey is a unique and special mission for them.

When we accept that we are spirit first and are part of the Divine Oneness, we take mastery of our destiny. Recognising that we are co-creators with the Divine, with the power and responsibility this entails, we move into fifth gear, the fifth dimension. Then we are able to travel smoothly along the road of life helping others on their way. We let go of our lower will and dedicate our journey to a higher purpose.

When we decide to relax and enjoy the journey we open the sun roof to let in the Light. That is Ascension.

Many people have fears and misconceptions about Ascension. Some think that it means rising up with their physical body, but this is not so. Two thousand years ago that was the case as the vibratory level of human beings could not sustain the frequency of Light, but we have now evolved. So do not worry about leaving your family. No one asks you to float out of the sun roof. At Ascension you stay firmly and happily in the driving seat, directed by Source, God, the Creator or whatever term you find acceptable for the Power in the universe.

At one time it was not possible to raise your frequency and stay in your physical body but now it is. Most people who now ascend choose to stay on Earth and serve humankind.

So if you choose to stay in your physical body on Ascension, you will live as you did before, but you will glow, shimmer and radiate at a higher vibration. Feeling joy, unconditional love and oneness with everyone, you will create for yourself Heaven on Earth.

You will be in planetary service, so your personal needs and desires will no longer be as important as your desire to serve All That Is.

As you become an Ascended Master your thoughts and words alone will create. Therefore you will be incredibly powerful.

In order to ascend you need to balance your karma from all previous incarnations. Karma is the balance sheet of your good and bad thoughts, words and deeds recorded over lifetimes. At the third dimension the consequences of low vibration action may not have to be paid back until a later lifetime, so there seems to be no correlation between your lifestyle and the hand fate deals you.

At the higher dimensions you must pay back debts more quickly. When your karma is finally balanced you receive instant karma. This means that if you have a negative thought or do an unworthy action, the consequence will boomerang back to you immediately. If you never seem to get away with anything in life, be grateful. You have reached instant karma and have the opportunity to keep your books balanced.

Every thought, emotion, word or action is on a vibrational frequency which attracts events, people and situations on the same waveband. Everything you send out, therefore, is brought back to you and ensures that outer circumstances in your life accurately reflect what is going on internally. It behoves us to look into the mirrors that are presented to us in life and change ourselves, not the reflections.

There are three exceptions to this:

◆ First, you may have past-life contracts which attract low-vibration people or circumstances. These contracts must be honoured.

◆ Secondly, you may have to face difficult situations and people in order to fulfil your chosen mission or destiny. This is why great spiritual teachers appear to attract dreadful traumas; witness the lives of many of the Great Ones of the past, including Jesus Christ.

◆ Thirdly, you may be receiving tests of initiation. Many on the Ascension pathway have completed their karma and are receiving these tests which are set by the Spiritual Masters to strengthen weak areas. They are presented to us as challenging relationships, financial situations or difficulties at work.

In order to ascend we first need to complete the mission we undertook for this life on Earth. Some people have an inner knowing that they are doing what they came in to do. Others may need to access in meditation the blueprint of their life. If you are not on your true life path, then it is important you take the decisions which get you onto it. Sometimes we have to take difficult decisions to ensure we are doing what we contracted to do before we came in.

A few years ago I was broadly on my path but I realised that I needed to make adjustments and could not complete my full mission until I changed various conditions. Soon after I made the changes I was told that there were certain colours not developed in my chakras over past lives. These related to the ability to make changes easily and to deal with finances. It was suggested that I take every opportunity to develop these colours over the next two or three years, so that I would be fully prepared for my mission.

I found that a tremendous help. It meant that when I was presented with considerable and consistent challenges I did not think, 'Help. How am I going to cope?' Instead I thought, 'Aha, this is another opportunity to strengthen myself so that I can do my work ahead.' My whole attitude altered and I became very much stronger.

People often say to me, 'I know I'm not doing what I came in to do but I have to stay in this job longer to get some money behind me.' I hear frequently, 'I know this isn't the right relationship but I don't think I can cope on my own.' I have been in all those spaces and well understand the fears. Yet the longer we procrastinate the slower our pathway. Sometimes I ask, 'How many lifetimes have you been stuck in this same test?' Often they say six or even ten lifetimes!

At Ascension the whole body turns to Light including your clothes. You then either return into your physical body to serve humankind at a higher level or you leave to serve out of your body.

At this time now on Earth there is an unprecedented opportunity to rise into the Light for there are waves of Ascension taking place. There are Higher Beings, archangels and angels, and great dispensations of spiritual energy available to help us all.

One essence of the Ascension pathway is co-operation. Few ascend in isolation. We are asked to hold the hands of our fellow brethren and move forward together.

You may be nearer to achieving Ascension than you think. If you wish to take advantage of the incredible opportunities offered now for the spiritual development of your soul, keep focused on your intention and desire to say, think and do everything from the highest and purest motives.

Lord Kuthumi, an Ascended Master, said, 'If only those of pure heart and mind knew how close they were to Ascension.'

We live in incredible times. Never before in the history of humankind has there been such an opportunity for spiritual growth.

This book offers you inspiration and information to help you ride on a wave of Ascension in this lifetime so that you can become immortal. You can leave the wheel of reincarnation. You can become a Lord of Light, an Ascended Master.

2: Meditation

When we are chosen for our place in Earth School we are considered, in universal terms, to be exceptionally fortunate. Many apply and few are accepted at any one time. Because we are at a time of great opportunity for growth, millions of spirits wish to incarnate now. We come on a mission of great difficulty, fully knowing that if we do not succeed we may have to start all over again. If we do succeed, the rewards are beyond our wildest expectations.

It is rather like being sent into the jungle. You are shown the map and given a precise briefing. Then the map is taken away but you are reminded that you have a two-way radio and must keep in daily contact with base. With constant communication you will be guided all the way and receive all the advice and help you need. Nevertheless you will have to negotiate the difficulties and dangers of the jungle and you must take important decisions for yourself.

Some people get into the jungle of life and forget to communicate. Others are too impatient to learn how the communication system works! Others listen and disregard the advice. Still more keep asking or even screaming for help and do not bother to wait for a response.

The two-way radio system is, of course, prayer and meditation. Prayer is our part of the communication. We are explaining our situation and asking for what we need. Now if you are in a tricky situation and are calling base for help and guidance, you expect to get it. And you do. However, most people pray for help in a mechanical way without any real expectation of response. It is more helpful when you are in a jungle talking to Source to state what is going on and what you need, and then ask for advice, knowing that there will be a response.

Assume there has been a response to your call for help or guidance and act as if the help you need is on its way.

Meditation is listening for the reply from Source. It is quietening the mind of all interference, so that you can get as clear a line as possible. All meditation techniques are aimed at stilling the mind.

For most of us, the response does not come as a verbal instruction in meditation, although of course it may do so if we have tuned in clearly enough. Sometimes a seed is planted into our mind in the silence. Then the seed, containing the information we need, grows bringing its ideas into our consciousness. At other times the response is sent through a book or TV programme. Sometimes someone else may say the words we need to hear or give us the information we seek. Occasionally a key is turned in our mind allowing access to coded information that was locked in our consciousness without our being aware of it. The help or answer may come out of the blue. It is our task to be receptive.

If you are in the jungle, cannot remember your instructions and do not use your two way radio, it can be a scary place!

Our mission is carefully discussed with us before we come to Earth and if we do not complete it, we have to come back and try again — at least we re-do the bits we did not successfully accomplish. If part of our life purpose is to deal with certain emotions, and we check out of our mission leaving relationships unresolved and emotions repressed or unmastered, we meet those same people and situations again. If we do not deal with our fears, we have to face them again. Some people have to pass through many pools full of crocodiles in their jungle.

Some people have been to Earth on many missions and are very experienced here. Others may have trekked many times in the deserts but have never tackled the jungles. Despite their great experience, life in the jungle may be extremely difficult for them. Still others will have climbed mountains, sailed the oceans and sledged to the North Pole but they get lost in the jungle.

In other words, there are some highly evolved beings amongst us who have had their experiences on other planets, in other galaxies and sometimes in other universes. Yet however evolved you are as a soul, if you have had little experience on Earth, you may feel strange or lost in life. Other planes of existence which you may have mastered do not offer the same sexual, emotional and financial experiences as this one. The material plane is the Everest of mountains to scale.

Many who are incarnating now have unfinished business, or karma, to complete and have agreed to do this at the beginning of their lives. When they have done so, they may have to train for a new pathway.

It seems to me that many are in that in-between stage. They feel the pressure of moving onto their new pathway but do not know how the steps to it may be accomplished. The answer is, of course, tune your antennae into a higher wavelength and listen for instructions. Then act.

As soon as you have completed your karma, your mission will be revealed.

SIMPLE MEDITATION EXERCISES

To do these exercises it is not necessary to see anything. Simply sense, imagine or feel and you will find yourself becoming more centred and able to access information for your highest good.

Exercise 1

1. Sit comfortably with your eyes closed.

2. Consciously relax by focusing on each part of your body in turn and asking it to soften.

3. Imagine you are breathing light into your navel, slowly and comfortably.

4. Allow your crown centre to open and golden light to flood your mind.

5. Raise your eyes to your third eye and breathe comfortably.

Exercise 2

1. Sit comfortably with your eyes closed.

2. Sense each outbreath stroking your body until it relaxes.

3. Imagine walking up a flower-lined path through green countryside.

4. Sit by a beautiful clear blue lake.

5. Quietly watch the calm water and feel the sun shining warmly on you.

6. Repeat 'calm' on each outbreath.

3: PURIFICATION

In order to be ready to ascend we need to be as pure as possible — mentally, emotionally and physically.

Negative emotions that we have not dealt with leave a residue in the cells of the body and in the aura and attract negative situations and people to us. If there is a relationship we have not forgiven or released, it is imperative to do the necessary work NOW.

If you are smiling on the surface, while burying resentment or hurt, quit pretending.

Spirituality is not about being sweet and nice. It is about being genuine and honest.

Only then can the murky pool of underlying negative emotions be acknowledged and dissolved.

If your emotions are turbulent or frozen, go into your still, quiet centre and ask for the core belief to be revealed to you. Underneath emotional imbalance there will be a belief from which your feelings generate. Once you reveal the underlying belief to yourself, you can make affirmations to change it.

For example, if your anger bubbles up from an underlying belief that it is not safe to trust weak men, you might affirm, 'It is now safe to trust myself and others'. If you find an underlying deeply held conviction that you always get it wrong, affirm, 'I always get things right.'

Through the wise, adult part of us, emotions flow freely. When they are blocked or out of control, a part of us is still stuck in childhood reacting to limitations. For example, a woman came to me who always felt sick when her boss started to get uptight. She was very capable at her job and knew very well how to placate her boss. Nevertheless she still felt sick when he sent out angry vibes. She was extremely sensitive to his states and realised that the moment he tensed up in a certain way, she unconsciously feared he would act aggressively, as her father had. Automatically she felt like the powerless child who used to be smacked, sent to bed or publicly humiliated. The old emotions, which were still stuck in her stomach, made her feel nauseous as she had done in the same circumstances when she was little.

To heal and reclaim her power with such men she learnt to care for and protect that stuck child within her. She did this by visualising the powerful adult part of herself standing up to her father and telling him he had no right to treat the child in that way. She also visualised him apologising to the child and telling her he was not angry with her but with outside circumstances. She pictured and felt her father cradling and loving the child. She did this consistently until the stuck part of herself felt safer. Then she was able to respond as a wise, mature adult to her boss when he was angry.

Immediately two more people magnetised into her life with the same angry energy and she was pleased to be able to handle them calmly and firmly without feeling sick. She knew then that she had learnt one of her life lessons and purified old stuck feelings.

So we also need to heal our stuck parts that still respond to old limitations. Try the visualisation exercise at the end of the chapter.

Emotions are physically expressed through the liquids of the body — tears, lymph, urine and saliva. Are these flowing freely and healthily or are you blocking the flow in some way?

Your physical body is your temple. Inflexible and

unreasonable mindsets will be reflected in tight muscles in your body. If you are tense, dance and move, shake your tension out, do relaxation exercises and visualisations, go for a walk in nature, laugh and sing, anything that helps you to let go, until your mind too starts to relax.

Physical purification also affects your spirituality. Kumeka, my guide, told me that chocolate and sugar, all dairy products and anything with a face or the product of anything with a face lowers our light. So do vegetables grown with pesticides. For purification we need to keep our bodily temple clear, exercised and cleansed.

When we leave Source we close down and the further away we move the tenser we get at a deep cellular level. When cells within us tense they are surrounded by density.

Imagine that a cell is like a light-bulb. In the centre of the cell is a filament which is our true twelve-strand DNA. If the light-bulb is connected to the electricity supply, then the filament glows. However in most of us dirt and dust prevent the connection. Also round each bulb are layers and layers of mud, or fear from past lifetimes. Wash the bulb and clean up the connection and the light glows.

The cells of your body are like a trillion light-bulbs. When you relax, purify and connect to Source, you are a powerhouse of light.

St Germain, an Ascended Master, a most incredible Illumined One, has recently obtained for us the Violet Flame of purification. It is yet another dispensation from Source to speed our process into the Light. When we ask for the Violet Flame and visualise it, purification takes place to the level we will allow.

So if you are upset by someone or feel annoyed when they are around — call on the Violet Flame and picture yourself and the other person within it. It can help you to purify all your relationships.

If you have feelings you wish to cleanse, ask St Germain for help, visualise the Violet Flame and step inside it. If there is a difficult or negative situation around you, hold it in the

Violet Flame. In my experience whenever I have done this I feel very different and the situation or relationship subtly alters.

To purify your life hold everyone that you have ever wronged or who has wronged you in the Violet Flame.

A very powerful affirmation is 'I AM the Violet Flame'. This connects your mighty I AM Presence to the Violet Flame. In some spiritual disciplines your I AM Presence is known as the Father in Heaven or the Monad.

I talk in detail about Archangel retreats in a later chapter. However, if we need purification, we can ask to be taken to Archangel Gabriel's retreat in the etheric at Mount Shasta, California. We can do this in meditation or at night. We know when some purification work has taken place because we wake with dreams about it.

The first time I asked to go to Archangel Gabriel's etheric retreat, I dreamt of an old situation in my marriage. In the dream I was lying on the floor twitching and jerking as all the old crystallised emotions were pulled out of me.

The following night I again asked to go for purification and this time in my dream a young woman walked down steps into a place where there was a fire. Suddenly there was a flash of golden light and when I rushed over to it, all I could see was a little pile of ash. Clearly some transmutation had taken place!

Fire is an important cleanser. Unhelpful or rigid mindsets cause us to worry, which surrounds us in a grey energy. Write your limiting beliefs on a piece of paper and burn them.

If you have angry thoughts about someone, write down your feelings or draw a picture of the person — and burn it. If it is impossible to use fire, tear the paper into tiny pieces and flush them down the loo or bury them in the garden. Do it with energy and the intention of letting it all go. Keep doing this until you sense the negative emotions have been transmuted. Monitor your thoughts on the subject and you will know how much you have purified.

Healers, counsellors and those sensitive souls who take in other people's problems need constant purification. It helps to visualise a shower or waterfall washing over you. Alternatively, when you are in the bath or shower, picture the water washing away all negativity. Imagination added to action is very powerful.

Remember that darkness serves the light and fear serves love.

Once when I was being subject to psychic attack, Kumeka guided me to burn old photos and to release my anger and frustration by constantly writing down my feelings and burning them. He told me to draw a picture of the person who was attacking me and burn it. Under his direction I cleansed my home, clearing out clutter, redecorating and sprinkling holy water in every room. I checked that there were only spiritual books on the shelves, for they radiate a pure light, kept candles and joss sticks burning and constantly played the eternal Om.

I dreamt that boiling water was being thrown against the golden dome round my house but could not penetrate it. When I had purified myself and the whole house in this way, I had a vivid dream that the person who had been attacking me was searching for me but could not find me. Purification had rendered me invisible.

Kumeka in his wisdom reminded me, 'Look how he has served you. He has forced you to purify.'

So we can bless the darkness. It serves us on our path to Ascension.

PURIFICATION EXERCISES

To release the stuck part of yourself

Your wise, golden, unlimited and adult self is always free. All negative emotions come from a child part of you, stuck in old feelings.

1. Close your eyes and take a few breaths to relax.

2. Think about the last time you felt angry, hurt or in any other way negative and let the feelings surface.

3. At that moment, ask yourself, 'How old was the stuck child inside me?'

4. Recognise its fear and pain and let your adult self give it whatever it needs to feel safe, happy and free.

5. Remind the child part of you that now you are there to look after it.

6. Breathe in golden wisdom and fill your aura with it.

Physical steps for purification

◈ Burn all relevant photographs or objects holding memories of the person, place or situation.

◈ Write down all feelings of frustration, anger, hurt, fear, etc., and burn the paper, flush it away or bury it. Repeat as often as necessary.

◈ Draw and label a picture of the person and burn, bury or flush it away. (A stick figure will do.) Repeat as often as necessary.

◈ Clear all clutter from every room of your home.

◈ Clean and if necessary redecorate your home inside and outside as appropriate.

◈ Check there are no books in your bookshelves or pictures on your walls that have negative energy. Surround yourself with plants and high vibration books, pictures, colours, etc.

◈ Sprinkle holy water in all rooms.

- Smudge with sage and/or burn joss sticks.

- Play sacred music and sing Om or chant.

- Put fresh flowers in your rooms.

- Cleanse and purify your crystals and dedicate them to the Light.

- Light candles.

Visualisations for purification

- Hold the person or situation in the Violet Flame.

- Invoke the help of the Ascended Masters, the Great White Brotherhood, angels and archangels.

- Psychically disconnect from the person or situation by visualising all cords which connect you and cutting them.

- When you are ready to do so, forgive the person, people or situation.

- Affirm, 'Divine Love and Light flow through me whenever I think of........'

- Bless the person or situation for offering you the opportunity for purification.

4: FREEDOM

When we are attached to a person, thing or emotion, we are imprisoned as surely as if we have a ball and chain round our feet.

If you saw a bird trapped in a bramble bush, you would undoubtedly release it so that it could fly free. If you saw that same bird in a bush and realised it was trapped not by thorns but by its fear of flying, you would be surprised; you would certainly free it and try to persuade it to fly.

We are incredible, amazing beings trapped in the chains of repeating patterns, rigid mindsets and emotional beliefs. It is time now to free ourselves from mental and emotional chains so that we can ascend. Unlike the bird, we do not have to wait for someone else to free us. The keys lie within us.

Most of us are attached to our friends, lovers, families, homes, work and a million other things. While this is humanly understandable, nevertheless it keeps us anchored to a lower vibration.

Awareness is freedom. The higher we go, the wider the overall picture we can see, and the greater the understanding we have. If you ask a mite on an elephant's back what an elephant is, it will reply that it is a grey, flat creature. To a flea, who can hop a few feet higher, it is a grey creature, covered in hairs like trees and pores like craters, while to a bird in the sky it is one creature in a herd of similar animals. From a spaceship, it is a dot in a country on Earth, which is one of millions of planets in the universe.

Some humans are purely in the third dimension. They believe only in what they can see, hear, touch and prove. They are like the mites on the elephant's back. Anyone whose world is limited to the material and physical is riddled with fears, doubts and illusions. To see with restricted vision and beliefs is to limit your power of creation. The material, physical world is known as the plane of illusion.

When we decide to move to a spiritual plane, previously unseen doors start to open. The fourth plane is the plane of unconditional love. Here we accept that we are spirit and become aware that we create our reality.

Each one of us is responsible for creating our reality. Our thoughts, words, emotions, willpower and actions direct our life and when we totally accept this, our life changes. We begin to understand the overall mission of our life. Then we can unlock our prison doors and fly free.

We are moving into a fifth-dimensional planet. In 1997, the fifth-dimensional chakras are descending into everyone (see chapter 13). When we activate them, we are totally identified with spirit and take full mastery of our lives. Our soul energy descends into the part of us that is incarnated, so we can live with joy and radiance, totally free of the old imprisoning emotions and beliefs.

The difference between a Master and a third-dimensional human is that the average person is tossed about like a leaf in the wind by the stronger wills of other people. Because most people need acceptance, approval, acknowledgement and love from others, they subjugate themselves to the will of those others.

Every time we need outside validation we are dependent on others, for we have given someone else authority over our soul. When we keep seeking advice and help instead of listening to our intuition and making up our own mind, we hand our power over.

Independence offers freedom.

Independence means listening to our intuition and acting on it — no matter what. It is approving, loving and acknowledging our self. We then radiate a wisdom and serenity which is totally charismatic.

The releasing of negative emotions brings freedom.

Most of us are anchored into the third dimension by chains of anger, hurt, lust, greed, pride, jealousy, etc. We are unconsciously saying, 'I prefer holding on to this old hurt to ascending,' or 'I would rather hold on to my proud aloofness than ascend,' or 'I choose to hold on to my fear of failure rather than to ascend.'

Sarah and Jack were two of the world's beautiful people. They were attractive, successful and very much in love; however, they kept having rows and arguments, for they were in a power struggle.

On learning that he had not invited her to an office function, even though wives and partners were invited, Sarah was devastated. On a rational level she understood his patterns, for his ex-partner had caused scenes in his office. But all her inner child insecurities and fears of not being good enough surfaced. She went round looking, sounding and feeling hurt.

I asked her if she loved Jack and her response was that she really did love him and more than anything else she wanted the relationship to work. She looked quite taken aback when I pointed out that that was not quite true. In fact, she wanted to hold on to her hurt more than anything else. To her credit she agreed immediately. She asked what she could do, for she still felt terribly upset. I suggested she reassure and empower her inner child. Only when her inner child felt safe and happy could she talk to Jack with a different energy. She did this and ten minutes later they were communicating as adults. He gave her genuine validation, which her hurt child would never have dragged out of him. She looked radiant and the hurt evaporated. When they connected at an adult level, of course he wanted to take Sarah to his office function.

The keys to freedom are:

◆ Forgive yourself and others. Send out the intention of letting go.

◆ Act as if you cannot possibly fail at anything you do. With success as the only outcome, what are you now free to do?

◆ Be serene. When you are centred and serene, you are detached and independent, no one can influence you.

◆ Place yourself and others in win–win situations.

◆ Creatively imagine yourself free, joyous, loved and successful.

◆ Be aware of and take care of your inner child.

Exercises

◆ Reflect on the following statement: 'Now that success is inevitable, what will I do?' (This applies to every area of your life.)

◆ Become aware of the thoughts, emotions and beliefs that stop you from achieving or receiving this success.

◆ Picture the thoughts, emotions, people and situations that hold you back as links in a chain. Cut out each link. Alternatively you can draw the things and people that hold you back and then erase them, cross them out or cut them up.

◆ With passion, energy and creative imagination, visualise yourself enjoying what you want in life.

5: INNER PEACE

When you are at peace you radiate a vibration, the quality of which allows all around you to feel safe.

When you are tense and anxious, you send out a subliminal message that all is not well, that there is something to fear. Others around you respond unconsciously to this message. Either they buy into your fear and increase it or they distance themselves, leaving you feeling isolated. Tension separates you from the Divine within and problems often appear insurmountable.

When you find the deep pool of serenity within, all the tension in your body melts, all fear dissolves. You are open to the Light and solutions to challenges present themselves. Doors open and life flows.

In a state of calm, peace and serenity you are like a rock. No one can hurt or anger you for you do not allow them to. Because they know this, no one tries.

Every single moment of life offers an opportunity for spiritual growth. This is because we are constantly thinking and every thought raises or lowers our vibrational frequency. A Master observes his thoughts, knowing that he creates the aura around him. At any given time, if you are anxious, you can stop and focus on calm thoughts and imagine positive outcomes to your challenges. You can picture a serene place. Your mind does not know it is imagination. It believes all is well and relaxes your body.

Words create symbols. Every word you utter has a shape. It may be an ice cube, an alarm clock, a golden cloak or a rose. Do your words freeze, hurt or frighten others or do they strengthen, heal and comfort them? Start watching the symbols you send out to others, for they boomerang back to you and stay in your aura, where they attract more of the same, because other people will unconsciously respond to them.

Silence is a profound spiritual practice.

Of course, actions speak even louder than words or thoughts. Ascended Masters do as they would be done by, so they cultivate caring, kindness, generosity, acceptance, courage and high-quality actions.

Humans often talk nonsense. They gossip. They talk of war, disease, hate and other rubbish. Unfortunately, many tend to think any other conversation boring.

If you wish to be a Master, do not buy into negativity, for there is another truth. Talk of hope, of light, of the wonders of the universe. Fill your conversations with inspiration. Seek the good in others. Acknowledge kind deeds and accomplishments.

Sense your aura becoming more radiant and peaceful by the minute.

If you wish to find inner peace bless your enemies. We are all one. We are all part of the Divine. Our enemies come to us as our greatest teachers. When we quit blaming and start to bless others our light glows and the serenity within deepens.

To be at peace we must take full responsibility for our life. We cannot be at peace if we give another the power to hurt or anger us, to frustrate us or make us feel jealous. If we blame anyone for what their actions have done to our lives or for how we feel, we are victims. Victims live in the third dimension.

A Master says, 'This has happened. How have I allowed it into my life? What is the lesson?' and does something about it. One person's lesson may be to love and accept a person or situation. Another person's may be to speak his truth with clarity; another may need to challenge or even to fight for her rights. Each must go within to understand the tests as they come and handle them appropriately.

To a Master every situation just is. The dog dies, a baby is born, a loved one is injured, the house burns down, you win a prize, there is a problem at work. A third-dimensional human reacts with rage or fear or elation — moods swing according to circumstance. The fifth-dimensional human stays centred.

We are humans and humans have emotions. Masters do cry. Masters do get angry. Jesus wept. Jesus was angry with the moneylenders. We cannot expect to be different. It is OK to mourn or grieve or rejoice. However, Masters quickly return to equilibrium. They do not expend energy swinging from one extreme of emotion to another.

Fear is the great robber of peace. Fear is an absence of love and light. It is a servant reminding us to raise the vibrations of our thoughts about that issue. Masters welcome and face fears, for they are opportunities for growth.

If you find fear staring at you, pray or fill your mind with mantras. Pray for the qualities you need. Pray for positive outcomes. This keeps you focused on the higher vibration and tells the universe you are ready to move on.

Once you have faced a fear, learnt what it has to offer and raised your vibration, you will never face that lower-vibration challenge again.

If you feel tension starting, which is the disconnection from God beginning to take place, deepen your breathing and slow it down. Deep, slow breaths reconnect us, for it is not just oxygen we are taking in but prana, which is the Divine life force. We are breathing the breath of God.

This is why breathing in cigarette smoke kills the spirit and why living in a polluted place destroys the life force. If you feel dispirited, take yourself to a place of beauty and clean, fresh air. Then breathe in God again. After any trauma or problem, Masters can bring themselves back to equilibrium again in three breaths. This is something to practise.

6: SIMPLICITY

While I have been writing this book Kumeka has constantly reminded me that simplicity is a key to Ascension. Each time I ask him for complex inform-ation about the Spiritual Hierarchy or something involved, he asks, 'Why do you want this information?' I am often obliged to agree that it is of mental interest and does not assist my spiritual growth. Sometimes he gives us the information, sometimes not!

On one never-to-be-forgotten evening, Shaaron and I were meditating together and linking to him at the higher level that we can achieve when we are together. Shaaron said that Lord Kuthumi had joined Kumeka and they were consulting together. Once more Lord Kumeka reminded us that simplicity is a key to Ascension.

At one point I asked a question about Jesus, the Christ, and Kumeka with his usual direct simplicity said, 'Ask Him yourself.'

Shaaron, who is totally psychic and often sceptical, gasped, 'Would you believe it if I said Jesus is here in the room with Kumeka and Kuthumi?' It was amazing! Jesus answered my questions and then picked a huge white daisy with a golden centre and handed it to me.

He then motioned for us to follow and took us on an incredible inner journey. We were encouraged to step through a portal onto tall white daisies. We had to trust totally that they would support us. Kumeka then took over and led us on to a temple where the Ascended Masters meet to be taught directly by God. Kumeka told me I could have one question and one question only and I would be given an answer.

I knew my question immediately. 'How best can I serve God?'

He handed me a scroll from a great library of scrolls. The answer was stunningly simple. 'Be still. Be yourself.' Further down it added, 'Then doors will open.'

A few days later at the spring equinox a group of us stood on a local hill top, a power spot, in the darkness of early morning. We were on a point where Saturn was in a direct line with Stonehenge. The Hale-Bopp comet, portender of immense changes, was bright in the sky. Then the sun rose, clear, brilliant and breathtakingly beautiful, one of the most wonderful sunrises I have ever seen. It felt like a gift, a reminder that nature in its simplicity offers us unbelievable beauty.

I had wanted to write this chapter the day before but things were too hectic. I had to be stopped in my tracks and reminded by the sheer silence and beauty of that early morning sunrise about simplicity. All things happen in God's time.

I heard a story on the radio once about an elderly woman who had spent years trying to feel God's presence. She went to one learned person after another in her search for God and tried all sorts of practices. One day she was chatting to a young vicar and she told him of her quest. He said hesitantly, 'I really don't think I can help you but why don't you go home to your little room where all your treasures and memories are. Just sit there with your knitting and look round at your memories and say thank you for all of them.'

'I'll try that,' she replied. 'It's true I have lots of bits and pieces in my room and they all have memories attached to them.'

She went home and sat down in her rocking chair with her knitting and as she clicked away with the needles she looked round the room and remembered many things. She said thank you for all the experiences and good times she had

had. After a time it seemed to her she felt warmer, kind of golden and peaceful. She sensed a presence around her.

She went back and told the new young vicar that after all her seeking and searching she had at last felt the presence of God as she sat quietly knitting in her home and being grateful. The simplicity of gratitude opens us up to God.

I asked Kumeka about ways to connect with higher healing. His response was typical. 'Go back to basics,' he said.

'Ask and the door will be opened. People seem to want to make things complicated when they are very simple. Simple desire is sufficient. Follow that with commitment in time and space and everything you truly desire will be brought to you. But you must ask. Some of life's greatest lessons are in the Bible. In this case remember the door without the handle. Knock and it shall be opened to you.'

He continued, 'Lots of people make an enormous living out of wonderfully complicated ways of doing things. It is not necessary. Human intelligence takes the simple and makes it complicated.'

I woke up one morning to find I had written on the pad by my bed, 'If it is complicated, it's from ego. Spirit is simple.'

So here are a few simple basics for life:

◆ Eat simply.

◆ Live simply.

◆ Bless your food.

◆ Enjoy everything you do.

◆ Be innocent. This means be in your essence. Do not try to be anyone you are not. Just be yourself.

◆ Constantly remember if someone is not acting from love, they are asking for more love and give it to them.

◆ Be still.

Exercise — To find the simplicity of the child

1. Sing or hum a simple song or hymn from your childhood.

2. Close your eyes and ask someone you admire — a Saint, an Ascended Master, any Holy Person — to come in.

3. Imagine them touching your head and blessing you.

7: ABUNDANCE

In the third dimension poverty consciousness is endemic. People are constantly thinking, talking and acting as if they were poor and lacking. They are affirming poverty. The media add to this by focusing on fear and loss, so confirming the belief now held in the collective unconscious that we are victims, helpless in a terrible world. As a result many people worldwide are creating a physical reality of poverty.

In order to live in the fifth dimension and then ascend we must embrace abundance consciousness.

This means breathing, thinking, talking and acting as beloved children of God, knowing we will always be supported.

Poverty consciousness comes from past-life vows of poverty, from unconsciously held beliefs in unworthiness or from conditioning by society that somehow it is impossible and unspiritual to be abundant. The opposite is true.

God wants all of us to live in abundance.

Abundance is flowing with love, happiness, prosperity and success, which naturally results in vibrant good health.

Prosperity is not having money in the bank, hoarding it for fear that it will be taken away or that there will not be enough. That is being mastered by money.

Prosperity is having plenty, knowing more will come. Prosperity consciousness is believing that there will always be plenty and thinking, talking and acting on that premise. Then we master money.

Love is not holding on to friendships and relationships or manipulating and blackmailing others to keep them by you. It is not making people dependent so they will not leave you, or pleasing others so that they will like you. Love is being true to yourself and enjoying your relationships with partner, family, children and friends, letting them be free, knowing there will always be people loving you. It is about caring unconditionally for people. It is also about loving yourself and feeling comfortable in your own company.

Success is not driving and striving for outside recognition and material things. It is a feeling of fulfilment and self-worth, of peace, joy and satisfaction.

Happiness does not depend on how other people treat you. Happiness is a sense of lightness and joy within.

Abundance flows as a result of your thoughts and actions. Let go of fear that there is not enough. There is plenty for all.

If you give something away while thinking, 'I'm always bailing him out,' or 'I always pay,' you are withholding. Generosity is a fifth-dimensional quality and means giving away freely from your heart. This ensures more will flow in.

Would you give more to others if you trusted more would flow in? Then give from your heart and it will.

Unconditional love is, of course, a fifth-dimensional quality. It means accepting people exactly as they are without judgement. It is acknowledging the good in others. It is compassion, empathy and understanding. Genuine love is such a magnetic quality that anyone radiating it draws people to them.

Would you let go of any of your friends or even your partner if you knew that the gap would be filled by higher-vibration people? Are your work, your hobbies, your home fully satisfying? Do they bring you a sense of joy and fulfilment? Is there anything in your life you would change if you knew that something much better would flow in? The fear that keeps you holding on to the old is blocking your channels of abundance.

Just as a river flows unceasingly, so the Law of Flow ensures that there are no voids in life. If we let go of something or someone, new things and people take their place, though there may be a waiting period. Naturally if you let things go and you continue to send out the same subliminal messages, you will get back the same old conditions. However, if you have let go of a lower vibration and you are now sending out a higher vibration, something new and better will automatically arrive on your doorstep.

A young woman who had been through a series of awful jobs with difficult, authoritarian bosses and several demoralising relationships had decided to work on her own personal and spiritual development. After two years of work on herself she was in a job where her boss and colleagues were light, relaxed and, more importantly, valued and respected her. Her new boyfriend was gentle, wise and caring. However, she was bored with her work.

She told me that she was applying for new jobs and feeling very confident about it. She said to me, 'I know I have mastered the old pattern and, having drawn in such lovely people to work with once, I can do the same again. I feel I can move on now to more fulfilling work.' Clearly she knew she had raised her vibrations and was ready to attract a more abundant job.

Abundance is deciding what we want and being totally clear that we deserve it.

Abundance is giving with the right thoughts, words, emotions and deeds. It is also receiving with the right thoughts, words, emotions and deeds. Because of the Law of Flow we cannot do one without the other or we block the river of abundance.

At the third dimension what we give out returns in some way.

At the fourth dimension what we give out returns three-fold. At the fifth dimension what we give out returns tenfold.

The Law of Tenfold Return

Whatever we give from the heart is returned to us in some way tenfold. We may give a meal and receive a book from someone else. We may give money to one person and receive a holiday from another. We may give someone a helping hand and get special nurturing from someone else.

Never expect something back from the person you give to. It negates the Law of Abundance! And receive everything that comes your way openly with a sense of deserving and gratitude.

You then have the key to greater 'wealth' than you have any idea of. You are a Master, for you are now operating the Law of Tenfold Return. This law, like all other spiritual laws, is exact.

What you give from your heart without counting the cost is returned to you in some way tenfold.

In order to live in abundance we must naturally love ourselves and give to ourselves. If we give to everyone except ourselves, it is time to question our motive for giving. We are usually over-compensating for our lack of love and self-worth and naturally this blocks the law from operating. So do not overgive to others. Keep a balance in giving and receiving.

If you get cross because you are supporting someone, pause and go deep into yourself. Are you rescuing this person? In other words, are you emotionally co-dependent? Or are you honouring a past-life agreement or commitment?

For example, I am sure Vincent Van Gogh and his brother made a pre-life contract that his brother would support Vincent financially in order that he could bring his incredible paintings into the world — paintings which I understand resonate with the vibration of Christ consciousness, hence their enduring popularity.

Unconsciously we may 'remember' that we have made a past-life contract to help someone at some point in their life. If we do not keep our promises, contracts and commitments made in this life or in a past life or even made between our Higher Selves, we will draw frustration, disappointment and loss into our life. When we honour these promises, we are rewarded tenfold.

A friend of mine helped a man through a terrible trauma in his life. She took him in, and supported and nurtured him. Yet from time to time she felt really angry that she was keeping him, for she feared she did not have enough for both of them. She resented always paying for him. Her business kept suffering setbacks.

Gradually I noticed her attitude towards him start to change subtly. She told me she did not mind supporting him financially any more, for she realised how much he supported her emotionally. As soon as she made this shift her business started to flourish.

She had been honouring a past-life commitment to him automatically and from the wrong space. While she did so she suffered business losses and holdups. Now, as she honoured the contract with her heart, she activated the Law of Tenfold Return.

Watch the manifestation of the Laws of Abundance in your life for it is a key to spiritual development.

Think of the Illumined Ones who chose lives of affluence and power. Kuthumi was Pythagoras and Shah Jahan, the Emperor of India who built the Taj Mahal. Serapis Bey was the Pharaoh Akhenaten. Monka was the head of the Inca civilisation. El Morya was King Solomon. When Jesus was Joseph, he became Governor of Egypt.

Once they had mastered the Laws of the universe, they chose to incarnate in positions of affluence and power, so that they could directly influence the lives of millions.

When lightworkers everywhere hold the money and power, the world will quickly transform.

Exercise — Abundance visualisation

1. Relax.

2. Open your heart.

3. Picture someone you dislike receiving exactly what he or she most wants.

4. Picture someone you love receiving all that he or she wants.

5. Picture yourself receiving all that you want.

6. Remind yourself that you deserve this and are entitled to enjoy it.

8: Manifestation

In order to ascend we must master self, in other words, our thoughts and emotions. We have discussed abundance, which is created by the positive direction of thought, word, emotion and deed.

A Master must do much more. He or she must also be able to master matter. By raising your vibration to the frequency of the Divine, you can control the formation of matter.

You can do it not only on this planet but in other galaxies and universes and become a Master Creator. This is a highly important work for those who have passed their tests of initiation and are ready.

Most will master the Laws of Manifestation on this planet first but there are those of you who came in encoded to help also on other planets and who will do much work there. You will be valued and rewarded in the Great Scheme of Things.

The basics of manifestation are to master the mind and emotions. All things at the higher levels come back to this. Devote yourself to the highest. When you can discipline your mind and emotions and focus them with clarity and intent, you will manifest with power and wisdom.

You are like an archer with his bow and arrow. Only stray thoughts stop your arrows of manifestation from reaching their goal. If you are easily deflected by the opinions and comments of others, you waver. You do not set your sights firmly and the arrow plops to the ground or misses its target completely.

Masters set their target. Their minds calm and clear, their emotions steady, they aim and nothing and no one can deflect their arrow.

The arrow itself must be straight and true. This is the intention. Intentions must be of the purest and highest. The feathers must be balanced and well trimmed. These are the emotions, the confidence, trust, sense of rightness which ensure a true flight.

The average person has a mind which is all over the place. The Masters keep their mind focused on the goal until it inevitably comes about.

Once you have a clear intention that the greatest desire in this lifetime is Ascension, to do the will of God, to leave the wheel of rebirth, to serve with the Masters at a higher level, then life becomes simpler. Choices disappear. You flow in a higher stream of consciousness.

Here is a great secret. When you wish to manifest a thing, a person or a situation into your life, you focus on the *higher qualities* this manifestation will bring to you. Imagine you already have what you want to manifest and feel the feeling of enjoying this higher quality already. By the Laws of Attraction this draws whatever is appropriate to you.

If you wish to work with healing, for instance, you focus on the joy and satisfaction, the compassion, the grace you have to offer. Suddenly someone will give you healing crystals or teach you to channel healing. Because you are flowing with a stream of Divine consciousness you know that whatever manifests is for your highest good.

If you wish to manifest a holiday, think about the sense of relaxation, refreshment, stillness you need, or if you prefer excitement, the adventure, exploration and change. This, with a clearly directed focus, will magnetise the perfect holiday into your life.

For manifestation at the higher dimensions you hold intentions for the highest good and leave the details to spirit.

An elderly widow whom I have known for many years longed for a man in the house. She wanted security and male companionship but at the same time to maintain her freedom. She really did not want another partner. She was very aware of what she wanted and sent out a pure note into the universe. She focused on drawing towards herself the qualities of security, companionship and personal freedom.

Within a few days a young male student knocked on her door out of the blue looking for digs. She would never have thought of taking a tenant but she trusted the wisdom of the universe and what manifested proved to be a perfect solution.

One of the keys to manifestation is the 'as if' principle. This is faith. It means acting as if you already have what you wish to manifest.

A young Polish couple wanted to emigrate to Israel and to live in a certain town where they could get accommodation and a grant to study. Their flight was booked but the papers did not arrive. A few days before the flight the papers still had not come and relatives were phoning from Israel and Poland full of doom and gloom. All were worrying, saying, 'Oh dear! Whatever are you going to do?' or 'How terrible! They'll never come in time,' and making all manner of negative, worrying statements, until the young couple were beginning to feel doubt and fear creep in.

Then the young man realised that they were doing it all wrong and that the negative energy was blocking the papers. He became very affirmative to the universe. He phoned all his relatives and told them that everything was fine, the papers had come and they had been offered exactly what they wanted. The tension dissolved. Everyone relaxed. The energy rose. At that moment the universe released the papers which arrived two days later in the nick of time. The couple had been given what they asked for.

Faith manifests.

You can manifest many things with the left brain alone. By working hard, driving, thrusting and striving, you can create material things but they are not balanced with the qualities of the highest dimensions, like love, trust and service.

Focusing on material things usually disguises a sense of emptiness. Furthermore, things can be taken away from you. Qualities you earn stay with you, for each time you earn a quality you raise your frequency and add a note to your harmonic range. You then transmit your tune containing that note and automatically draw to yourself more of what you wish to manifest.

When you pass over, no one is interested in the material wealth you have accumulated. The pursuit of wealth is considered wasted energy. However, the lessons you have learnt in managing money are assessed.

The qualities you have earned in a lifetime are your wealth and stay within your soul vibration for all time.

In the third dimension manifestation requires clarity about your goal, focus of mind, emotions and willpower, plus action to make it come about. It is essential to do something.

In great civilisations such as Atlantis, where the vibrations were much higher, it was only necessary to focus the mind, the will and the emotional energy on a goal for it to manifest. No other action was necessary. Many lightworkers are remembering this and omitting to take action to bring their visions into reality.

The higher we raise our vibrations, the less necessary action is. In the fifth dimension will, thought and emotions alone are enough to manifest.

9: DISCERNMENT

All lightworkers and those wishing to follow an Ascension pathway must listen to their own intuition at all times. Intuition comes not only in flashes of knowing, but also in feelings of enthusiasm and excitement, a sense of rightness. Masters never rely on external advice, only on intuition.

We instinctively know what the energy of a person or situation is even if we can't quite put our finger on it. The first instant impression, before our rational thinking mind takes over, is so often the right one. If you sense something is moving too fast for you, call a halt. If your gut feeling is that something is not quite right, check it out. People often say to me, 'I just knew they were lying but I did what they wanted anyway.' Trust your inner voice or handle the consequences.

As a Virgo, discrimination and discernment have been major lessons throughout my life. I look back in amazement and laughter at some of the choices I made without following my intuition.

Many years ago, before anyone had ever heard of Reiki, I was so bowled over by meeting a Reiki master, who claimed to be a plumber handyman, that I got him to install a new bathroom in my house, solely on the grounds that he was a Reiki master and must therefore have a good energy. Did I regard the fact that he was on the dole with no intention of working (very bad karma), had abandoned his wife and young child without emotional or financial support? No. Did I take notice that he told me he had bought his Reiki mastership cheaply because he was on the dole? No. Did I check out his credentials as a builder or plumber? No. 'How fantastic to have a Reiki master to install my bathroom,' I thought.

I paid the karma for that lack of discernment with weeks of trouble. He took the old bath out and left it at the bend in the stairs for six weeks. When he finally arrived to remove it after more phone calls than I can count, he said, 'It's no wonder the bath got stuck here. I sense there's bad energy at this point in the house.' Having come to my senses, I was able to point out that the bad energy was a result of the frustration we all felt as we squeezed past the bath on the stairs.

If I had used discernment I would have followed my original instinct and found a reputable plumber.

It is OK to discriminate about who you invite into your home or your life. Discrimination is not judgement on anyone. Would you want a thief as a friend? We can honour someone on their pathway and still take a decision that we do not wish to be connected with their energy.

Many lightworkers feel they are being judgemental when-ever they say no. Often, healers and therapists cannot turn away someone who comes to them for help, so they get overwhelmed by the heavy energy of those who seek to drain their light.

All energy has a vibration. It is up to you to discern the energy of those around you and then discriminate about which ones you wish to have in your life or you wish to work with or treat.

Cults, religions and most governments dictate what people do or think. This severe control and limitation holds people back. It took a group of warrior women to incarnate, who were prepared to sacrifice themselves for what they be-lieved in before women in Britain were allowed to vote. Those women knew what was right for them and were prepared to act, no matter what the consequences.

A Master must be independent and take his or her own decisions. Until we can discern what is right for us we cannot take mastery.

This is the danger of cults and religions. When we let someone tell us what to believe or do, we become puppets. The mass suicides of young cult members which have hit the headlines over the years are tragedies which have resulted from individuals giving their power away to someone who is dark, in other words, separate from God. More wars have been waged, and killings and tortures perpetrated in the name of religion than for any other reason. In every case the leaders have been working for the darkness and their followers have not used discernment.

Religions can also be a source of great goodness, light and spirituality.

There are countless paths to the top of a mountain and there are many mountains which we can choose to climb. Beyond all the mountains are the sun, the moon, the stars, the heavens and that is where we are aiming.

Jesus Christ said, 'There is only one way.' He meant that the only way to return to Source is through Christ consciousness. This is through opening the heart and living in unconditional love and acceptance of all humanity. Christ consciousness is the way. Without living in Christ consciousness we cannot ascend. All the intellectual knowledge in the world is pointless unless the heart is open.

To become a fully ascended Master you must become a fully enlightened Buddha, the mind energy, as well as a Christ, the heart energy. Love and wisdom are brother energies.

If children and adults were given permission to speak their truth and taught to follow their intuition, then honoured for doing so, there would be no war. Hitler could never have gained power. People who follow their inner guidance become peaceful, happy, fulfilled people.

We are all being bombarded with information and channelling from all sorts of sources. Some people tend to read or listen to it all and believe it all. This can be incredibly confusing. Not everyone brings through information from the highest source and it is up to us to use our powers of discrimination to take in only what feels intuitively right to us. Darkness not only feeds false or inaccurate information through less than pure channels. It will often very subtly distort the truth which leads to the confusion and doubt it desires. Bear in mind that no one in a body can ever be totally pure, so with the best intentions in the world all channelling is distorted through our own programming.

Do not be influenced by someone else's perspective. Stop thinking someone else must know more than you or must be right. Even if someone says they are channelling Source or Jesus Christ or a mighty Archangel, even if they have two degrees, have talked to aliens, written a dozen books, held workshops, appeared in the media, if what they say does not feel intuitively right for you, let it go.

Any teacher of the Light will say, 'If what I say resonates with you, accept it. It is for you. If it does not resonate, let it go. It is not for you.' If months or even years later it resonates, *then* it is right.

No one has the right to say, 'This is the truth,' for no one has the whole picture while in a human body.

Also consider that all the channels may be right from their perspective. Imagine a huge bowl of fruit. Looking at it from one angle you can only see the bananas, apples and cherries. From the other side you can see plums, pears and the bananas. From above, the little cherries at the side may be hidden. Each person describing what they see is correct and yet none has the overall picture.

As a lightworker you were trained before you came to Earth. You have incredible knowledge and wisdom stored within you. Open up to who you are and trust your own intuition absolutely.

Some of the entities trying to communicate are mischievous or stuck. There are many who have passed over but have not evolved. If they have no scruples or understanding they can pop in and give you information or guidance which is misleading or plain bad. If you did not trust Uncle Charlie when he was in a body, why do you think you should trust him just because he is dead? He can say he is an Angel of Light if he likes or a high guide. It is up to you to discern whether the energy of the communication is right.

Your aim is to connect with a Being of Light who is at a higher level than your Monad or at least your Higher Self. If they are not, you would be better to listen to your own Higher guidance.

In our planet of free will, where there is light there is also darkness. So for every Angel of Light communicating with you, there may be a dark angel. For every pure light guide working with you, there is its counterpart in the darkness. It is up to you to discern and discriminate.

Because of this situation of duality on Earth, one of the spiritual laws governing our planet is the Law of Challenge. This states that if we challenge any being or entity three times in the name of God and all that is Light, then they must truly declare themselves or depart.

The higher Beings of Light welcome challenges. It means that we are being conscious in our efforts to discriminate.

If you have any doubt about where your guidance is coming from, say or think, 'In the name of God and all that is Light, are you ....?' Wait for an answer. If it is 'Yes,' repeat your challenge twice more, each time waiting for a response.

I have never experienced this — but if the answer is 'I am,' listen very carefully in case they quietly add, 'not'. It is better to ask for a yes/no response.

When you have received your reply and wish to go ahead with your communication, it is totally appropriate to ask what their purpose and intention is in contacting you. If you have any doubt whatsoever during the channelling or connection, stop and challenge again.

Then relax and enjoy the process of communicating with a higher energy, always accepting only what feels intuitively right for you.

10: PROTECTION

When you are on the spiritual path you are like a person carrying a lamp, walking along an open pathway. The good news is that the light of the lamp shows you your way and lights up that of others. The downside is that you are visible and vulnerable. Anyone of lesser intent who does not want you to spread light or who wants some of your energy knows where you are.

There are many, including governments and religions, who have an investment in keeping people in fear and confusion. Authoritarian regimes and individuals are themselves very afraid. They control and dictate from fear, need and greed. They feed on the fear and confusion of those they control and it gives them a feeling of power. The last thing they want is for individuals to feel relaxed, clear and independent.

Yet the new Golden Age is beginning to dawn and before long the facades of the old ways will crumble. As the energy of co-operation comes in people will no longer feel content to compete or do someone down. Life will become a team effort. Everyone will help to bring out the best in each other so that everyone gains. However, until everyone has the highest intentions towards their fellow beings, we need protection.

I have always believed that the best protection is an open heart, but we are physical, emotional, mental and spiritual beings and any disharmony in any of these four bodies will cause us to be vulnerable, so that darkness and confusion can enter.

When we are physically, emotionally, mentally and spiritually strong then we are impregnable.

Darkness consists of anything of a heavy vibration such as fear, jealousy, anger or depression. When brooding, malevolent, critical or angry thoughts and emotions are directed at you, They can penetrate your weak or vulnerable areas like arrows. Very often they serve to take away your clarity and fill you with confusion. Then you doubt. You cannot be a Master and you cannot move forward on your spiritual path.

The mirror technique is very powerful. Someone who attacks you with bad thoughts can make you feel anxious or ill, and you may not understand why. Put up a mirror facing towards them to return the missiles to their source.

I was the subject of negative psychic attack by someone who wanted to put out my light. He was consciously attacking me with his thoughts and energy. I put up a mirror between us, facing him, while at the same time a friend of mine sent him love. The attacks stopped. I asked which had been more effective and was told that the mirror had stopped him. Kumeka said that the man had unconsciously seen his own darkness in the mirror and been shocked by it. So if dark people are attacking you, imagine a mirror deflecting back their energy. You can also send them light. Light contains spiritual information and knowledge which must dissolve the darkness.

A woman I know was frequently ill. Kumeka told me that her daughter hated her and constantly directed black thoughts to her. She was unconscious of this and did not want to know it, believing that her daughter loved her. Without telling her it was her daughter who was psychically attacking her, I suggested that she put up a mirror to protect herself. She did this and immediately felt much better.

If you are ungrounded, you are vulnerable. The biggest vulnerability, however, is fear. The old adage that there is nothing to fear but fear itself is very true. Someone who is sitting at home terrified, worried and anxious about everything is vulnerable to their own and others' dark thoughts. If you are weak-minded and easily influenced, you are psychically open, a sitting target for trouble.

Those who are strong-minded, calm, relaxed and happy are impregnable. When you are dancing, having fun and laughing, you are a source of despair for anyone wanting to attack you psychically. They can't get a hold on you.

If you are dedicated to walking the Ascension pathway it is important to clear yourself out. Make sure you are physically strong and healthy by following the physical laws of good food, fresh air and exercise, rest and relaxation.

Suppressed or denied emotions block your chakras, while wild out-of-control feelings leave you open and out of balance. The aim is to flow emotionally by honouring feelings and expressing them as you feel them. This keeps your emotional body pure.

Your mental body reflects your thought forms and patterns, so the Masters observe their thoughts, if necessary seeking the underlying beliefs and removing them.

The greatest protection is serenity. Are you in harmony with your spirit? Do you feel satisfied and fulfilled in life? Do you have time to relax and enjoy the beauty of the world around you? Are you happy to be on Earth? In order to ascend we must be able to relax and enjoy the flow.

A client I knew very well, called Jenny, was on a fast path of spiritual growth and she had cleared a great deal of debris that blocked her aura. However, her throat had always been vulnerable to infection and often she could not speak out when she needed to. She had started to notice that she would sit with her hand over her mouth, as if it was a physical impediment to her speaking.

She wanted to explore and heal the source of this blockage, so she allowed herself to relax quickly and easily into a light trance where she could access the memories she needed to look at. She slipped into a past life when she was a man at the head of an army. As a commander he had led all the people who believed in his higher teachings into a massacre. He was taken alive, then taunted and ridiculed by his captors, until he began to doubt his own truths. After languishing in prison he was offered release by poison. Jenny, as she relived the experience as that man, contorted with pain as the poison burnt the back of the throat.

She was aware that all those who followed her in that life were members of her family now and realised that she was afraid to speak in case it led to disaster.

As she gained this awareness I could see a black energy looking like a dark, prickly hedgehog in her throat. Angels appeared and stroked it until it became a golden ball of wisdom. One of the angels said to her, 'You can speak with wisdom now.'

It speeds our Ascension pathway when we are ready to look at and release the blockages in our aura. Jenny will no longer be so vulnerable through her throat chakra.

Nothing happens by chance and as I am writing this chapter a friend, whom I will call Heather, has phoned. She is in the process of separating from her husband who is going back to his own country. Not surprisingly she has been feeling very unwell and unsettled and had decided to fly out to stay with him for a week soon after their separation, thinking that would help.

Heather said, 'I have just had a phone call from Jean, my psychic healer friend, who is picking up that my husband is being used by the dark forces to psychically attack me. How can this be and what can I do?'

Heather is a therapist and lightworker but like all of us has her own issues to work through. Her husband, while very charming, is also very angry with her. I am sure he sends her brooding, angry thoughts which the forces of darkness can latch on to. This dark stream of energy focused from her husband then penetrates her broken aura. If she were not a lightworker, the darkness would not be interested in trying to stop her work.

I suggested she invoke the gold ray of Christ regularly and start a thorough process of purification. When she has purified herself and her home, she will be impregnable. I reminded her that ultimately the darkness is serving her higher purpose by forcing her to protect and purify herself.

I also asked her to consider that the darkness attaches to her husband's thoughts, so while he is focusing on her, it can wreak its havoc. Once they are separated, her husband's thoughts will be less directed towards her, so the impact of dark energy will lessen. If she visits him, his old angers will probably resurface and, unless she is purified and protected, will penetrate her aura again. She decided not to visit him until she felt stronger.

Here are some powerful protections. Remember a protection is only as effective as you believe it to be. If you believe your protection is one hundred per cent then it is.

The blue cloak

Deep blue is a very protective colour, the colour of Archangel Michael, who is the protector. With your imagination draw in your aura and then put a deep blue cloak over it. Pull the hood over your head and zip the cloak up from under your feet to your chin. Feel and know yourself to be completely protected.

The golden egg

Ask the angels to put a golden egg of light around you. Make this a thick golden band of energy. Then visualise or watch them putting a dark blue energy round that. Finally, especially if you work with people and often pick up their problems, place a violet colour round the outside, which will keep you safe from the negative energies of others.

The gold ray of Christ

One of the most powerful and protective of all energies is the gold ray of Christ. It must be invoked three times. You can either call it forth yourself or ask your Monad or your mighty I AM Presence to invoke it. Add, 'It is done.'

For example, 'I now ask my Monad to invoke the gold ray of Christ for my total protection.' Say this three times, then add, 'It is done.'

A tube of light

Call down a tube of light from your mighty I AM Presence to protect you throughout the day. Ask that it remain intact and be divinely charged, so that nothing that is not of God and the Christ-Light may pass through it. You may also ask that the Divine Light transmute all negative conditions within you to positive.

Your angel

Always ask your angel to protect you. In asking, you strengthen the link between you.

11: FINDING YOUR MISSION

Your higher purpose, in other words your pathway in life, is that which gives you a great sense of joy and satisfaction. If you feel enthusiastic, alive and inspired you are on your path. So when you do what gives you a great sense of fulfilment *and* are not prepared to settle for less, you are fulfilling your purpose.

There are other clues to your mission.

Less highly evolved souls have many paths they can choose. There are always more infant school places than opportunities for doctorates. The evolved soul will prepare and choose its mission with great care and will be ready to wait until the time and circumstances are right.

This means that before you incarnate you will seek the date and place of birth as well as the parents who can offer you the most important opportunities and lessons.

Astrology can give you a great deal of information about the life path you chose. A good astrologer can give you insights about past lives as well as current destiny. More simply, how do you feel about your particular birth sign? If you have never thought about it, think about it now. How do you feel about the place where you were born? How do you feel on your birthday?

Every sun sign has a lesson attached:

◆ Fire signs — Aries, Leo, Sagittarius: Giving divine, outgoing, all-embracing love to others.

◆ Earth signs — Taurus, Virgo, Capricorn: Staying grounded and giving service to others.

◆ Air signs — Gemini, Libra, Aquarius: Embracing brotherhood. Everyone is a brother or sister.

◆ Water signs — Cancer, Scorpio, Pisces: Clinging to your centre of peace no matter what, so that your wires do not get jangled with the emotions of others.

Numerology is the science of numbers. Each number has a vibration and numerologically your date of birth will give you information about your life path.*

At a spiritual level we recognise that the incoming soul telepathically imparts to its mother or father the name it wishes to be known by. Each letter of that name has a vibration and so the name itself has a vibration. We live in a universe of vibration, like attracting like. Therefore experiences and lessons are drawn to us every time our name is spoken.

Many choose to have an abbreviated name or a nickname in childhood, only drawing in the full vibration of their lessons in adulthood. My experience as a child is a common one. I was called by an abbreviated form of my name but when adults wanted to express displeasure or disapproval they used my full name. This practice implies to sensitive children that their full mission is difficult or even dangerous.

If you do not like your name, it does not necessarily mean that your parents were not listening. It is more likely to mean that you do not like the lessons you chose!

If you do not resonate with your name, it is important to understand why you don't. If you do, it may indicate you are comfortable with who you are and your destiny.

---

* For more information about numerology see *The Power of Inner Peace* published by Piatkus.

Both my daughters decided to change their Christian names at the same time. According to my guidance they wanted to avoid their lessons at that time. Later my guide informed me that my older daughter, who changed to her middle name of Dawn, was now bringing in a more psychic, spiritual aspect of her destiny.

Some people I know have completed what they need to do with the lessons called in by one name and as soon as they change their name, their life path subtly changes. When a woman takes her husband's name on marriage, a new vibration enters her life.

Because children are so much closer to their soul energy, the childhood fantasies we had often give us a clue to our mission. The child who wants to be a nurse may be expressing a desire to serve or heal. One who yearns to be a mountaineer may well become an explorer or may be registering a soul longing to be a pioneer or to be a spiritual leader. The little boy who aims to be a train driver may be recognising a desire for leadership and to be in command of something big.

Our parents are the ones who launch us on our mission. They are the commanders who set us off on our path, even if they abandon us or abuse us. They are vitally important choices.

You came in to Earth as a being of light to learn from and overcome your parents' bad qualities and to embrace their good ones. This is an important part of your life task.

For example, if a parent was weak and non-supportive, your task is to overcome weakness and strengthen yourself until you become independent.

A critical parent indicates a lesson of valuing yourself and others. A pushing, driving parent suggests part of your purpose is to learn balance. A stubborn, pigheaded parent may mean that you have to learn tolerance but you will also have the opportunity of developing tenacity.

An abusive parent indicates that your great mission is to love unconditionally. Childhood abuse can sometimes be used as a basis for developing healing ability and it is also a challenge not to abuse others in your turn. Some brave souls even pass through abuse and neglect as a test of initiation which will give them the necessary experience to bring other abused people through into the Light.

If your parents were absent or disinterested, they launched you on a pathway to be self-motivated or to do things alone.

The wonderful qualities of your parents were for you to absorb and enhance in yourself. Generous parents help you to be open-hearted, courageous ones to be strong. If you chose warm, loving, supportive parents you will have a good grounding to be able to create strong relationships to support you on your life path.

So your parents equipped you for your mission. What tendencies do *you* have to overcome? What soul qualities are *you* developing?

Major fears that you have in your life are like dragons on your pathway. They stop you moving forward and block your clarity. Even if you escape them by taking another route you will still have to face them sometime! Remember, fear serves love. Tune in for guidance and overcome your dragons.

Every experience you have had up to this moment of your life is preparation for the pathway ahead.

While it is wonderful to know that you came in with a mission to be a nurse, a healer, or a captain of industry, or for a specific purpose such as drawing the attention of the world to the plight of the dolphins, it is not strictly necessary to know what your mission is. Just ask in meditation each day to be shown the next step and doorways will open until your destiny becomes clear.

Exercises

◆   Sing or chant your full name lovingly. Do it aloud and put as much caring into it as possible.

◆ Sing or chant your full name lovingly while looking into your eyes in a mirror.

◆ Even better, let someone else sing or chant your name lovingly to you. Keep eye contact and let yourself be as open as possible.

12: THE MONAD

In the beginning was the Om, the sound of creation, which has been translated as the word. Every culture has its own remarkably similar myth of creation and each myth contains the essence of truth.

This is how I understand the story of creation. The Creator is pure Love and Light, omnipotent and all wise. Yet pure Love and Light has nothing to test itself against. You cannot practise unconditional love, for instance, when you are surrounded by unconditionally loving people. It is too easy. There is no test and you cannot grow without facing challenges. Without darkness Light cannot compare itself. So the Creator wanted to expand and experience.

He/She created twelve universes and then sent out billions of sparks of His/Her own energy, each with a special mission, in order to experience. These original sparks are called Monads. They are of an incredible brilliance and light, a wonderful vibration of love. The plan is that these Monads will return to the Godhead when their mission is accomplished, rather like children returning to the family home to share wisdom and experiences and so enrich the family.

However, the Monads in turn needed to experience and grow in order to fulfil their missions, so they each sent out twelve souls. These are what we know as our soul or Higher Self. Then the souls decided to expand and experience, each sending out twelve extensions, stepping down the vibration, so that denser matter could be experienced. You are one of those soul extensions.

This means that, for instance, one aspect of your soul might be in Saturn, another in Venus, a couple in the Pleiades. Some of your total energy might be resting back in the soul or be in between incarnations but you will all be psychically connected.

Some souls even decided to send emissaries into the free will zone of the universes to experience dense physical matter, which meant forgetting their origins — a truly frightening and dangerous undertaking with great penalties for failure and wonderful rewards for success. This meant sending extensions or aspects of the soul to Earth. Many came here and got themselves stuck deeper and deeper in density. Some reincarnated thousands of times in their efforts to free themselves from darkness, with which they had become deeply impregnated.

At this time of expansion more enlightened ones are incarnating to help with the great awakening. Some souls and Monads are sending several of their personalities here, so there may be other aspects of your soul or of your Monad here on Earth now.

At one time no one met another aspect of their soul while on Earth. This is no longer so and I know many people who have met others from their soul or Monad. Certainly I have met others from my soul, who have chosen to incarnate here at this special time to help in the big change of consciousness taking place. I also channel very often with Shaaron, who is from the same Monad. She is a spiritual cousin.

You have 11 soul brothers or sisters somewhere in the galaxies to whom you are closely linked, while there are 144 of you altogether from your Monad. The bad news is that, because you are psychically linked, one or more may be drawing on your energy. The good news is that you can help and support each other.

Years ago, before I understood any of this, I was at a talk. A woman in the audience said that she was always tired and did not understand why. The speaker tuned in to her and said that another aspect of her soul was taking her energy and, while this was not normally acceptable, in this case she had agreed at a higher level to offer her energy to help her soul sibling. The woman absolutely accepted this and understood that her energy was at that time an offering to another.

Normally it is not acceptable to let anyone take your energy, for it is a form of co-dependency. If you suspect that someone is pulling your energy, before you go to sleep tell them firmly but politely that you honour and love them but your energy is for you and you no longer give permission for them to take it. I learnt that an aspect of my soul was taking my energy and once I had severed the cord and told this person telepathically he could no longer have any of my energy, I felt a whole lot better.

When you have passed your third initiation — and you may well have done if you are reading this book, you link with your soul or Higher Self. Then you are guided by your Monad and are working on a much higher vibration. At the fourth initiation you merge with your Monad.

The Monad is sometimes known as the I AM Presence, or the Father in Heaven.

The fifth dimension is about love, equality and co-operation. Your soul group ascends together, so you cannot ascend until all the others are ready. Ascension is not about individuals forging ahead. It is about soul families (members of your Monad) and soul groups (groups of like-vibration people) moving forward together. We do not know who is of our soul group, so that person we despise or dislike may be the key to our all moving forward. Freely help and accept everyone. In many cases one of a higher vibration will willingly lead a whole team of people up the ascension ladder. Co-operation is the name of the game for Ascension!

13: Fourth-Dimensional Chakras

Chakras are spiritual energy centres, of which there are seven main ones in the body. Their purpose is to take in and transmute energy.

At the third dimension the seven chakras are the colours of the rainbow which, when spinning in perfect alignment, make white light.

The third-dimensional chakras

◈ *The first chakra*, the base centre, is red and monitors our physical, material survival. It helps us take action and get things done. Our life force or kundalini energy is stored here.

◈ *The second chakra*, the sacral centre, is orange, the colour of sociability and friendliness. It is our emotional and sexual centre and is linked into collective unconscious beliefs about sexuality. This is the chakra of clairsentience, which is the psychic ability to pick up someone's physical pain and draw it into our body to transmute. Most of us have experienced this when we have chatted to a friend who has a headache. We listen to their problems and they leave feeling fine while we go home with the headache. It can also pick up much deeper problems.

◆ *The third chakra*, the solar plexus, is yellow. This is our area of personal courage, confidence and willpower. If we want to control others, this is the chakra we use to do so. If we are afraid, this centre becomes a greeny yellow or liverish colour. The more confident, independent and wise we are the deeper the yellow. From here we constantly send out feelers to check that we are safe, for instance when we are driving the car. If we sense our loved ones are in trouble or danger, our solar plexus antennae reach out to search for information. Most of us hold fear in here from our childhood or past lives. In this case our solar plexus will tense if someone with a similar fear or anger is near us.

◆ *The fourth chakra*, the heart centre, is green with a rose-pink centre. If we hold on to old rejections, this chakra closes down. When the heart centre opens with compassion, love and empathy, we start to become healers and other people feel very safe and enfolded in our presence.

◆ *The fifth chakra*, the throat centre, is turquoise. It is the chakra of communication and is about speaking how we honestly feel and what we truly believe. When we are afraid to speak out or want to please others, we block this centre. A block here may manifest as a sore throat. A pain in the neck may literally mean that someone is being a pain in the neck and we dare not tell him how we feel. On a psychic level when the fifth chakra is open, we are telepathic, we pick up psychic impressions and listen to our inner guidance.

◆ *The sixth chakra*, the third eye, is deep indigo-blue. When our third eye is open, we are clairvoyant and psychic, and our healing ability is enhanced.

◆ *The seventh chakra*, the crown chakra, is violet and is our connection with our Higher Self.

◆ *The eighth chakra*, sometimes called the seat of the soul, is blue white and is related to our auric space. Through it we connect with our Higher Self or soul for guidance. It is located above the head and, as we bring down the fourth-dimensional chakras, it descends into the crown, where it temporarily doubles up with the chakra in the crown.

As we expand from third-dimensional into fourth-dimensional beings, the first seven chakras move progressively down the legs. Third-dimensional chakras are related to that which is physical or solid. Our fourth-dimensional chakras are both solid and light. They connect us on a personal as well as a galactic level. This means that when our fourth-dimensional chakras are open, we have the opportunity for intergalactic communication and work. Fifth-dimensional chakras are purely light.

When the first seven chakras move down the legs the next seven descend one by one taking their place. (The ninth chakra moves down into the base, etc.) Then we move into the fourth dimension and our personality self merges with the soul.

When the fifteenth chakra doubles up with the eighth, we take guidance and instruction from our Monad.

The fourth-dimensional chakras

◆ *The ninth chakra*, in the base centre, is a wonderful glowing pearl-white. This is the chakra of joy and as it begins to open, it ignites the light which is in the cells of the body. When we are grounded in joy and delight instead of survival, our whole attitude becomes one of trust and gentleness. We glow with light.

On a galactic level this chakra takes us outside the atmosphere of Earth. From there we connect back to Earth becoming one of its guardians. We are truly responsible beings.

◆ *The tenth chakra* in the sacral centre is a luminous pink-orange. As our masculine and feminine energies balance each other, this chakra starts to open, keeping us in a state of alignment with the soul.

Imagine an old-fashioned scenario where the man and woman had strict and opposite roles. The woman was creative, intuitive, artistic. She loved, nurtured and cared for her man. In exchange the man supported and protected her. He thought her inspirations through and then took action, ensuring that things got done. He provided and she received.

Take the man and woman out of this and call them masculine and feminine energies or yang and yin which is less confusing. Then recognise that these energies are intended to work internally in perfect balance and support. Our inner life is mirrored externally.

A perfect balance is when our yin side comes up with creative ideas and intuitions which our yang side supports and activates for us. While our yang energy is protecting us, logically deliberating and taking action, our yin side is nurturing, caring for and comforting us.

It is helpful to check how balanced we are.

Please take the time to reflect on the following questions:

- How are your relationships with the men in your life? Father, brothers, uncles, male boss, male friends?

- As a man, how do you feel about expectations placed on you to remain strong and yet nurture and care? How do you feel about being a provider?

- As a woman, how do you feel about expectations of holding down a job as well as being a wife and mother?

- The outside world and the world of work are represented by the masculine energy. What is your attitude to these worlds?

- How do you relate to money, power, politics?

- How do you give?

- Are you authoritative, controlling, assertive, dominant?

◆ Do you think too much? Are you intellectual? Do you rationalise, analyse and compartmentalise everything?

◆ Are you afraid of the future or do you want to rush head-long forward?

◆ Is the right side of your body relaxed and strong or is it weak, damaged or tense? (Our yang side is governed by our left brain, which is intellectual, controlling and out-going — any problems are reflected physically in the right side of the body.)

◆ How are your relationships with the women in your life? Mother, sisters, aunts, female boss, female friends?

◆ As a woman, how do you feel about expressing nurturing and caring in business?

◆ As a man, how do you feel about showing the vulnerable, caring and nurturing aspect of yourself?

◆ How do you feel about nourishing and healing others? Can you be tender, compassionate and wise?

◆ Do you honour your intuition? Do you let your creative and artistic side flow?

◆ Are you able to listen? Can you ask for help? How do you receive?

◆ Do you hold on to the past or do you deny it?

◆ Is the left side of your body relaxed and strong or is it weak, damaged or tense? (Our yin side is governed by our right brain, which is creative, intuitive and nurturing — any problems are reflected physically in the left side of the body.)

The activation of the tenth chakra enables us to reach into the solar system so that we can access information, send out light and love and participate more fully in the healing of the planet.

◆   *The eleventh chakra*, in the solar plexus, is pure, shim-
    mering, shining gold. Gold is the colour of wisdom. It
    signifies confidence and power. At the third-dimensional
    level the yellow solar plexus is a psychic chakra which con-
    stantly picks up the vibrations of people and situations
    around us. If we hold unresolved fears here from this life
    or past ones — and most of us do — then external fears
    or negative emotions will attach to our solar plexus and
    make us feel tense and uncomfortable. When the fourth-
    dimensional gold chakra opens, it holds no blocks to
    which external fears can attach. The vibrational waves pass
    straight through the chakra leaving us feeling relaxed, calm
    and wise no matter what the external circumstances.

The eleventh chakra is a galactic chakra. As this chakra
descends and opens it becomes important to meditate in
a group to link into other galaxies.

◆   *The twelfth chakra*, in the heart centre, is a pale, ethereal
    violet-pink. It is the total spiritualisation of the heart
    energy and opens as we enter enlightenment. The Christ
    consciousness is anchored here; so as this chakra opens
    we are living in unconditional love and automatically
    open the heart chakras of those around us.

The Aquarian Age is about living in the Christ consciousness.

This chakra links us in to the rest of the universe. I have
no information about the cosmic importance of higher
chakras.

◆   *The thirteenth chakra*, in the throat centre, is a deep blue-
    violet colour. When this chakra descends and opens,
    much higher psychic and spiritual energies become avail-
    able to us. We open our healing channels and are able to
    heal mental as well as physical conditions in others. We
    open up to many psychic gifts and are able to work with
    the Laws of Materialisation and Dematerialisation, using
    our thoughts as well as our power. Now we can commun-

icate with Archangels and Higher Beings. There is an immense sense of strength with this chakra.

◆   *The fourteenth chakra*, in the third eye, is a translucent golden-white. When this chakra opens our mind automatically surrenders to the Divine Plan. Our thoughts are of a higher, purer vibration. We truly are one with the Will of God. We can transmute the karma of others and are now open to the higher levels of clairvoyance and prophecy and are able to communicate on the inner planes with Masters and higher guides.

◆   *The fifteenth chakra* is white-violet. When this chakra descends into the crown we have merged completely with our soul, or Higher Self, and take our guidance and instruction from our Monad.

In order to open the fourth-dimensional chakras we must have passed the fourth initiation. This, for most of us, is like a crucifixion. So if you have gone through a crucifying time in your life it may well be that that challenge was the flame that burnt the dross of the old, enabling you to move into the fourth dimension.

I am told that the fifth and sixth initiations are easier. It is a process of purification and more purification, of filling yourself with light and then offering yourself in service to humankind — or whatever your particular pathway is.

The fifth-dimensional chakras

There are seven fifth-dimensional chakras — chakras sixteen to twenty-two. Kumeka has said that they are coming in for everyone now. I know very little about them.

◆   *The sixteenth chakra* is platinum. We offer service based on a solid spiritual foundation.

◆   *The seventeenth chakra* is magenta and platinum. This opens when we feel true Oneness with All That Is, with the plant and mineral kingdoms, with the brotherhood/ sisterhood of humankind.

◆   *The eighteenth chakra* is deep gold and rainbow. Here we
    are using wisdom and power in service to the Godhead.

If you meditate on these chakras you will identify with
their energy and therefore open them up into service more
quickly.

Exercise — Meditation to bring down the fourth-dimensional chakras

1. Relax into a meditative state.

2. Move your red chakra from your base centre into your feet.

3. Then the orange chakra from your sacral centre into your
    ankles.

4. The yellow chakra from your solar plexus into your calves.

5. The green chakra from your heart centre into your knees.

6. The turquoise chakra from your throat centre to above your
    knees.

7. The indigo chakra from your third eye into the upper thigh.

8. The violet chakra from your crown centre to the top of
    your legs.

9. Bring down your eighth chakra into your crown centre,
    doubling up with the violet chakra.

10. Bring down your white-violet fifteenth chakra into your
    crown.

11. Bring down your golden-white fourteenth chakra into your
    third eye.

12. Bring down your deep blue-violet thirteenth chakra into
    your throat centre.

13. Bring down your pale violet-pink twelfth chakra into your
    heart centre.

14. Bring down your gold eleventh chakra into your solar plexus.

15. Bring down your pink-orange tenth chakra into your sacral.

16. Bring down your pearl-white ninth chakra into your base centre.

17. Sit quietly radiating the new high vibration colours.

18. End the meditation by closing your chakras.

14: LIGHT LEVELS

The more light we have in our cells the nearer we are to Ascension.

In order to pass the third initiation we have to have a light level of 50%. Then we merge with our soul or Monad.

The light level for the fourth initiation is 62% after which we leave the wheel of rebirth. For the fifth initiation the light level is 75%. For the sixth initiation and Ascension we need a light level of 80–83%. To pass the seventh initiation and become a full ascended master we need 92% light level. It is then no longer possible to sustain a physical body.

I asked Kumeka what determines Ascension and he replied that we needed to maintain four weeks of consistent light level in the outside world. So it is no use retiring into a spiritual retreat where it is easy to keep pure.

I found the light levels rather confusing. Kumeka explained that the above percentages are levels of light when in the body. He said it was probably easier to say that as a spirit you can achieve 200%. For example, if your light level was 98% out of the body, in the body it would be half of that (49%). Incidentally you need to be at 50% light level in the body to go into the spiritual dimensions at night.

Here are some things that lower our light levels: gossip, greed, negative thinking, refusing to take decisions, laziness, overwork, unkindness, confusion, holding on to hurt, tension, anger, being in a hectic city, poverty consciousness. Consciously cut as many as possible out of your life.

And here are some things that raise our light levels: generosity and abundance, singing, laughter, being out in beauty and nature, serenity, love, clarity, relaxation, hugging from the heart, meditation, joy, decisions, thinking good of others. Consciously bring more of these things into your daily life.

Do be balanced about changing and purifying your life. If you wear a white robe in a dark room, the robe appears pure and clean. As you shine light on it the stains start to show. The brighter and more intense the focus of light, the more stains show up. So if you are doing a lot of work on yourself, a great deal is likely to surface. This does not mean you are a bad person, just that you are shining more light into your soul.

As we lighten our vibration so our unresolved stuff begins to emerge and be drawn to our attention. Childhood problems, old patterns, denied feelings and past-life traumas all come up to be looked at like spots and stains.

Lots of people on the Ascension pathway decide they will do everything possible to lighten their vibration unaware of the impact such a sudden change will make. Not only do they practise all the techniques offered in this book, but they also seek and search into their past not realising just how much they are stirring up.

A lady came to me in a state of breakdown. In her determination to clear and purify herself as quickly as possible, she had undertaken, in a brief space of time, an intense fasting and colonics week, Reiki healing twice a week, rebirthing, past-life therapy and bodywork. She had also practised prolonged daily meditation, yoga and talking to her spirit guides. On top of this she had read dozens of books on spiritual growth. She was in overload and simply could not cope with everything that came up and hit her. She had to take a long rest.

The path of balance is quicker in the long run.

When you move to a higher level of consciousness your karma is transmuted. Then your Monad sends tests of initiation to strengthen any areas that need to be tested. It is easy to feel deflated and that you are still being subjected to karma. You are not. Nor are you being punished.

All challenges and difficulties are either unfinished business, which is karma, or a lesson to be thoroughly learnt before you can achieve a higher vibratory level. You tell the difference by sensing within.

To raise your light levels and become a Master you must witness and monitor all emotions, thoughts, feelings, words and actions. As you watch how you react to challenges you may be surprised, even disappointed at yourself for a while. However, be sure that the test will return in another form so that, with awareness, you can choose a new response at a higher vibratory level. Each time you do so you are raising your overall light level and you are on your way to Mastery and Ascension.

After I had done a big piece of inner work, releasing and purifying old stuff, followed by a short physical detox under Kumeka's guidance, he told me that I could lift an old part of me out and release it. I would like to share the inner journey he took me on. It proved to be a powerful visualisation for me which you might like to do for yourself.

Exercise — Dissolving the shadow

1. Relax and let your whole body be comfortable.

2. Walk up steps to a magnificent cathedral or other spiritual place that feels right for you.

3. Sit quietly and absorb the atmosphere and energy of this place.

4. Visualise yourself lighting a candle.

5. Let the shadow you are ready to release step out of you.

6. Pick up the shadow part of you and dissolve it in holy water in the font or in pure running water.

7. Sense yourself shimmering and radiating light.

15: THE MAHATMA ENERGY

My understanding is that there are energies or vast Beings out in the universe to which we can connect if we know how. For example, many are now being initiated into Reiki energy to learn or in most cases to remember the ways to attune to this important healing force.

Another of these powerful energies is the Mahatma energy, also known as the Avatar of Synthesis, which is said to speed up our path of Ascension a thousandfold if we invoke it regularly. When I first heard of this energy a spark of excitement arose in me and I knew it was going to be tremendously important. To speed up your spiritual growth a thousandfold is amazing!

Apparently the Avatar of Synthesis contacted Earth in Atlantean times and said he would come again when we were ready to receive this energy. At the Harmonic Convergence, so many people around the world prayed and meditated for peace and spiritual growth that there was a response from the Godhead allowing the Avatar of Synthesis to reconnect with us.

This Mahatma energy is a group consciousness to which the twelve rays and a number of vastly powerful Beings contributed to create a great pool of energy into which we humans can now tap. Mahatma, as those who admire Gandhi well know, means great soul. This energy is accessible to everyone without exception. It is therefore available to you if you wish to meditate and invoke it.

Of course, according to spiritual law, if you wish to access this or any other help, you must invite it in.

The Mahatma energy is the highest of the energies available to us on Earth.

Despite its great power it cannot burn us out because it is stepped down through great Beings and then through our Monad and soul to the incarnated aspect. It is like a cosmic electricity power station and the enormous voltage, which would kill us if touched directly, is passed through substations before it reaches us at a much lower voltage.

It acts as a link between us and the Godhead. Many people believe that they are connected directly to Source and indeed this is a possibility for everyone. Sadly however, according to Kumeka, only a handful of people on the planet actually do connect with Source. Most who claim that they do are, in fact, connecting with an Archangel or their Monad.

Between the incarnated personality and the soul there are several steps or initiations, more up to the Monad and hundreds between our Monad and the Godhead. The Mahatma energy builds a bridge of light — or Antakarana — between us and Source. For the first time we have high-frequency cosmic help available to build our Antakarana to its ultimate destination.

Because of its high frequency, the Mahatma energy helps us to raise our frequency to that of Light, facilitating our Ascension process.

The Mahatma energy is golden white in colour, an indication that it is a very fine and high vibration. When we call it in, it flows through our physical, emotional, mental and spiritual bodies, in other words, through our physical body and our aura, and then into the Earth. It vibrates gently through our systems until our energy becomes finer. It helps to break up hardened and crystallised thought forms and emotional patterns.

Using the Mahatma energy is the most effective way of

balancing and re-energising our glands. Our glands keep us youthful and sexually alive, keep our immune system healthy and our metabolism balanced. The pituitary gland sends out hormones which will keep us youthful or, if we buy into the collective conscious belief in ageing, will make us grow old. When we ask the Mahatma energy to balance and re-energise our pituitary gland, it is important to ask the gland to send out life and rejuvenating hormones and to stop sending out death hormones.

The more of this Mahatma energy we, as incarnated souls, call down, the lighter Earth becomes, for the golden white vibration flows through us to heal and spiritualise the planet. When we access this energy, we use our power to accelerate Earth towards its Ascension. The more people who know about the Avatar of Synthesis and call on it, the more quickly the consciousness of all will rise.

I have told many about this amazing energy and led hundreds in meditations to access it. Many have had a similar experience to me the first time they have called it in — a feeling of being totally on fire. At other times it feels very gentle, like a flowing electric current but it is always powerful!

It can be invoked up to three times a day. This incredible energy helps build our light-body more quickly, powerfully and efficiently than has ever before been possible. Because it is such a high frequency our light-body becomes a cosmic or monadic body.

We can ask the Mahatma energy to help us with personal problems. We can mentally direct it towards anything that needs resolving. We can send it to others for healing.

Use prayer, meditation, visualisation and affirmation to invoke the Mahatma energy. Do call on it and tell everyone about it.

Here is a simple way of inviting the Mahatma energy to work with you. 'I now invoke the Mahatma energy to flow through my body and my aura, into the Earth, allowing me to use my life in service to the Divine.' You may visualise it as a golden white ray coming through and around you and then direct it wherever you wish.

According to Joshua Stone in *The Ascension Manual*, since the Harmonic Convergence with its Divine dispensation of the Mahatma energy, a human being could theoretically evolve from a second-degree initiate to a Galactic Avatar in one lifetime!

He suggests an invocation for the Mahatma energy given to him by Vywamus: 'I choose to accept and invoke a deep penetration of the Mahatma energy into my entire energy matrix, thereby allowing a full, open radiation of my Divine self in service to All That Is, now.'

Exercise — Visualisation for energising and balancing the glands

1. Relax.

2. Invoke the Mahatma energy.

3. Sense or imagine the golden white ray coming down from the Cosmos into your crown chakra. Ask it to relax, balance, energise and heal your pineal gland. You may visualise the gland as a small ball or in any way you prefer. Sense it being held and soothed in the Mahatma energy.

4. Move down to your third eye and flood the pituitary gland with Mahatma energy. Tell the pituitary gland to send out only rejuvenating hormones, which keep you young, supple, open-minded, healthy and vital.

5. Move down to the throat centre and sense the thyroid gland being soothed and healed by the Mahatma energy.

6. Repeat in the heart centre with the thymus gland.

7. Repeat in the solar plexus with the pancreas.

8. Repeat in the sacral centre with the ovaries or testes.

9. Repeat in the base centre with the adrenals.

10. Let the golden white Mahatma energy flow down your legs into the Earth, filling the Earth with spiritual energy.

11. Send it to anyone who needs it.

12. Close your chakras.

16: REIKI AND SPIRITUAL HEALING

There is a pool of Divine energy in the universe, which when accessed can be used to heal physical, mental, emotional and spiritual blocks. Those who can tune in to its frequency can direct it to other people, animals, plants, situations and themselves. It can be sent through time to heal the past or strengthen the future.

This is Reiki healing energy and there is a re-awakening in our consciousness to its power, so that more and more people are being attuned to receive it, while a few people are naturally able to tune in themselves. It is no accident that this energy is being unlocked now for us to access.

— *Rei*, meaning Universal, is the Higher Spiritual Consciousness, the all-knowing, omnipresent Godforce that can flow to the source of a problem. It restores harmony and fills us with light, automatically raising our vibration.

— *Ki* or *Chi* in Chinese, *Prana* in Sanskrit, also called *Mana* or *Golden Liquid Light* is the Divine energy that flows through all living things. This energy was a Divine gift originally made available in Atlantean times, when the symbols to access it were known by the priests and priestesses of Atlantis, many of whom are reincarnating now. It was used by Tibetan Buddhist monks thousands of years ago and was rediscovered in the 1800s by Mikao Usui.

Unless someone is born already attuned to the Reiki frequency or spontaneously finds the channel, they will need a Reiki master to tune them to the right frequency. It is as if we are television sets which need to be specially tuned by an expert to receive this particular station.

During a Reiki initiation both the physical and etheric body is tuned to a higher frequency. This allows a clear channel for the high-frequency Reiki current to flow through it. Each time a Reiki healer plugs into the source of the power, the current flows through, clearing the healer's channels, and then on to the place, situation or person to which it is directed.

Of course, spiritual healing does the same thing but the process and the vibration are different. With Reiki healing, people are attuned with symbols, which the master places in their crown, heart and hand chakras. During later attunements they are given symbols to enable them to access deeper levels of the energy. So the keys to tune into this power source are specific symbols.

Reiki healing energy comes down on violet light, which is the highest vibration we can see with our physical eyes and is the ray of purification.

A client of mine was very upset that various of her friends were being attuned to Reiki and even becoming Reiki masters, who could initiate others, without having a deep knowledge of healing techniques and a sense of devotion to the use of this great healing force.

I asked Kumeka about this and he said that some who knew how to plug into Reiki energy were technicians. There were also those who were true healers. Those who were technicians attracted people who needed technicians to initiate them. Those who were healers needed true Reiki healers to initiate them. It is logical, for everything follows the spiritual laws and like attracts like.

However, Kumeka did add that the true healers were much more powerful. You can imagine that if a technician is tuning in a TV set he follows the rules. Do this, turn that and it should work. If a person who truly cares that the set is properly tuned does the job, he takes time and trouble, uses intuition and a personal sense of commitment to make sure there is a perfect alignment and connection.

So as with all things, if someone decides to be initiated as a Reiki healer, it is important to use intuition to select the Reiki master who does the attunements. If you receive Reiki healing, it is also sensible to use your intuition about the healer you choose.

Like all received spiritual information and knowledge, Reiki has expanded and extended over the centuries. New symbols have been received. It is important to keep the purity of the healing vibration and the highest intention when accessing it.

A true healer brings through the Reiki energy with love and compassion, directs it only to that which is pure and for the highest good and uses visualisation to focus the power.

Soon after I had my Reiki II Initiation, I was quietly doing my morning yoga practice when a stream of consciousness came into my head. A voice said, 'I am Dr Usui. It is very important for everyone to raise their vibrations now and Reiki attunement is one way to do this. Be aware that many people are unconsciously remembering their past lives as Reiki healers or feeling attracted to Reiki. People are arguing about whether it is right to attune only healers — or technicians too. But it is beneficial for all. There are times when a technician is needed. Know that Sai Baba, the Cosmic Christ and many others are helping with this work. Know that Reiki angels, specially trained, are also helping the process. Reiki is an important part of raising the consciousness.'

The voice and information was so unexpected that I was taken aback but I report as accurately as I can remember.

Reiki energy, like all spiritual energies, cleanses and purifies the physical body as well as mental and emotional beliefs. It refines old, entrenched mental beliefs, so that rigid mindsets and unhelpful beliefs or attitudes are dissolved. The symbols work on the unconscious mind to dispel negativity.

Reiki healing works through the Higher Self of the person being healed.

The recent history of Reiki

Dr Mikao Usui was born in Japan in the mid-18th century. He was impressed with the Buddha's desire to help others, and noted that Buddha was said to be able to heal illness and that his disciples acquired healing abilities by following his teachings. He set out on a quest to learn about healing.

Whenever he visited Buddhist temples in Japan, he was always told that the spiritual side is more important than the body, and also that the ability to heal the physical is found when we focus on healing the spirit.

Dr Usui became a friend of the Abbot of a Zen monastery. Here he studied the Buddhist scriptures, the Sutras. He learnt Chinese in order to study them in their original language, then learnt Sanskrit so that he could read Buddhist writings never translated. That is commitment. In the Tibetan Sutras, written in Sanskrit, he discovered the formula for contacting a higher power that the Buddha himself had used.

At the end of a seven-year search, Dr Usui had the information he needed but not the ability to heal. So he decided to follow the formula and go to the mountain of Kori-yama to fast and meditate for twenty-one days. On the twenty-first day he saw a beam of light shooting towards him. He realised the light was going to strike him and thought it might kill him, but decided that the ability to heal was worth the risk. The beam struck him on his forehead and knocked him unconscious.

Rising out of his body, he saw bubbles of light containing symbols. He received attunement and knowledge of each symbol and was initiated into Reiki healing.

As he walked down the mountain he hurt his big toe. He held the big toe with his hands and in minutes the pain and bleeding had gone.

At the foot of the mountain he stopped at an inn for food, his first for twenty-one days. Although the innkeeper warned him not to eat so much after such a fast, he ate a normal meal but felt no adverse effects. The innkeeper's daughter's face was swollen with toothache. He used the Reiki energy to heal her.

After that Dr Usui spent seven years in a beggar camp in Kyoto, healing the sick. When they were better, he sent them off to find work, but they came back saying it was easier to beg than work. He realised he was being a rescuer rather than a healer, so he left and searched for those who longed to be healed. When he found true seekers he taught them to heal themselves and gave them the principles of Reiki to heal their lives and thoughts.

He gave master's attunement to sixteen people including Dr Chujiro Hayashi, a retired naval officer, who was charged with keeping the essence of Reiki intact after Dr Usui's death. Dr Hayashi opened a Reiki clinic and as a result of his further research, he created the hand positions, the system of three degrees and the initiation procedure. Dr Hayashi passed the complete Reiki teachings to Hawayo Takata, in order to preserve them.

Hawayo Takata was the daughter of Japanese immigrants living in Hawaii. She went to Japan to receive medical treatment for a tumour but in the hospital, as she was being prepared for surgery, she heard a voice say the operation was not necessary. At that late stage she refused surgery and was taken to the clinic of Dr Hayashi. Four months later she was completely healed and asked to learn Reiki. She stayed with Dr Hayashi for a year then returned to Hawaii.

He visited her there to help establish Reiki in Hawaii and initiated her as his thirteenth and last master. She introduced Reiki to America. Feeling that the Japanese concept of respect and devotion was difficult for western minds to accept, she decided to charge a large sum of money for the Reiki master attunement and training in order to create an appreciation for Reiki. She initiated twenty-two Reiki masters including her granddaughter Phyllis Furomoto, who succeeded her as Grand Master, which she still is. Both Dr Hayashi and Mrs Takata added to the original system to ensure progress.

Dr Mikao Usui lived by these principles:

- Just for today do not worry.

- Just for today do not anger.

- Honour your parents, teachers and elders.

- Earn your living honestly.

- Show gratitude for everything.

Spiritual Healing

When our heart centres start to open we feel the desire to heal others. Then we start to raise our consciousness and learn to open up to Source, so that we channel healing energy. We go through a process of gradually clearing our channels so that the healing energy flowing through us becomes stronger and clearer. We step the Divine healing energy down through our own chakra system so that it is perfect for the person we are healing.

The vibration is obviously different from Reiki healing; so some people will be attracted to spiritual healing and others to Reiki healing. All is perfect. Everyone draws to themselves what is right for them, and more diversity and opportunity is now being offered.

Many spiritual healers work on the aura, in which case the healing can take place in the spiritual, mental, emotional and physical levels. Hands-on spiritual healing tends to work on the physical body only.

Healing with angels

When you call in the angels to heal through you, amazing things happen. They lift the consciousness of the healer and the person being healed to God.

17: Wake-Up Calls

Marji had led a conventional life, married to an ordinary, somewhat controlling man. She had three adult children. She worked as a physiotherapist at a hospital and, because she had no spiritual understanding, she worked on bodies mechanically, as though they were cars. Boredom had begun to set in.

Spirit simply had not entered her life. She had never even heard of spiritual healing. However, when it is time to wake up the higher powers have their ways of attracting our attention. In 1991 the fateful weekend arrived for Marji.

Her husband and son were away at their weekend cottage. She arrived home from work to find their house had been burgled, but not just robbed The whole house had been desecrated. Feeling totally shocked and violated she called her daughter and the police. She felt she must tell her husband but she did not want to tell him on the phone. So she and her daughter jumped in the car and drove to the holiday cottage.

There another shock awaited her. Far from asking her what was wrong, before she had a chance to speak, her husband shouted at her for invading his privacy. She and her daughter drove home without telling him about the burglary.

The next day, feeling desperate, she wandered with her daughter round Glastonbury, enveloped in a black cloud. Her eye caught a sign which read, 'Spiritual Healing'. Until that moment she would have ridiculed the concept but to her amazement she found herself thrusting her bag into her daughter's hands, saying, 'I'm going to have some healing.' Her daughter gasped, 'Mother, you can't', but Marji turned and walked into the clinic.

Fate had arranged that the last appointment at 4pm was free and she found herself sitting opposite a man she trusted immediately. She relaxed as she felt calm and peace flowing from him. She told him what had happened and that she had not yet told her husband about the desecration of their home.

The healer took both her hands in his and looked into her eyes. Immediately she felt a fantastic sensation. A shower of light came out of him and streamed all over her. Both of them were enveloped in indescribable light. She said, 'We were at the core of the light and it was spinning round us. The light felt like pure compassion. I had no idea of time.'

Marji left the clinic feeling shell-shocked and felt a compulsion to buy a Bible, which she started to read as well as all sorts of spiritual books. From that moment she stopped reading newspapers and watching TV. She felt she had moved into a different world and was constantly thinking about that wonderful event. She kept remembering how it felt to be in the light.

When eventually she told her husband about the light, he said she had been hypnotised and must snap out of it!

Desperate to find out more about the light, she went to see a local vicar who said he was very busy and she should see a psychiatrist! Instead she went on retreat and read more books.

After her experience Marji's patient-load at the hospital immediately doubled. Patients did not want to see anyone else. They all asked for her. She was radiating light and healing power.

A year later she went to visit her brother, an atheist, who lived abroad. She had altered so much that he asked her what had happened to change her so. She told him that she had had a spiritual experience on 29 October 1991. Marji expected that to be a conversation stopper and indeed it proved to be. The discussion ended abruptly.

To her surprise on the following day, when they were alone, her brother approached her and said, 'I want to know what happened to you.' She told him the whole story and about being enveloped in the indescribable light.

He then told her that on that same day he had been sitting in his apartment on his bed with his gun across his legs. He intended to kill himself. At 4pm he suddenly thought of Marji's children and how dreadful it would be for them. He put his gun down at the moment Marji had her spiritual experience in the light.

The incredible story does not end there. A few weeks later Marji met her soulmate. He was a down-to-earth working man, a plumber, who had never had a psychic or spiritual experience. They fell headlong in love and embarked on a passionate secret affair. He told her that a most extraordinary thing had happened when they met. He saw a radiant woman behind Marji pushing her towards him.

For four years they loved each other with joy and passion. Marji felt herself open up and flower as a woman. Then suddenly he lay dying in her arms and she was plunged into total desolation and grief.

Because she was married she could not talk to anyone, so she went away for a week's holiday on her own. In despair and depression one evening she walked alone down a dark street. Suddenly she saw a light and then the whole street lit up. She stood alone in this great light thinking, 'There is life after death.'

When the light left, she felt wonderfully lighthearted. For the first time in her life she walked into a bar alone. A man at the bar told her that he was a lifelong atheist but when she entered he thought God had walked in. They exchanged addresses and he writes to her frequently and describes how now he sees God in everything.

The Divine Light can enter and set us free from the darkest of prisons.

In Greece I was talking to a man in his late thirties. As soon as I met him, I knew he had great wisdom and suspected he had been an Initiate. It transpired that despite his wisdom he had abused drugs, which had opened him to the dark side.

This is the story as Simon told it to me.

'I had a friend called Dick. We were hippies together and he was always the life and soul of the party. I assumed he had it together and was happy but one night I was walking home in the dark when I saw a figure sitting on a wall sobbing. It was Dick. He told me he felt alone and unhappy and I comforted him, but I could hardly believe this was the Dick I knew.

I went off travelling again but I was lost and miserable and spent most of my time stoned. I got in with a coven of witches who were using indiscriminate power. Life was a dreadful nightmare. After a particularly horrendous happening I knew I must get away. I escaped and went south.

One day, outside a nightclub, I felt something reach inside me and tug me into the club. Inside was one of the witches from the coven. I tried to ignore her but the power was too much. I was drawn into the web and entered hell again. There was no love. I stayed in hell for another two years.

Then one day I bumped into Dick, who was by now a Quaker, and we went for a cup of coffee. He realised I was in deep distress and said to me, 'You have to remember that love is the crowning of the Moksha.'

I asked, 'What is the Moksha?'

He said, 'It's the spiritual path.'

I felt as if an axe split through my head into my heart. It hurt so much I thought it was killing me. I told him what I felt and cried out, 'What's happening?'

He laughed and replied, 'It's love, you idiot.'

I was in shock but left hell. I had been there for seven years. At last I was happy and at peace.

However, after a few months I indulged in drugs again. Next day a voice from nowhere spoke to me. It said, 'So high as you have been, so low will you go.' I plunged back into hell again.

Two years later I still felt terrible. One night I had a near-death experience. My guardian angel stood in front of me and said, 'You're here now. Do you want to stay or go back? If you go back it won't be easy.'

However I took the decision to come back and work through the darkness. I can tell you it hasn't been easy.'

Initiates who give into temptation go deeper into matter (hell) than those who have never aspired to walk on the spiritual path. Hence the words spoken to Simon, 'So high as you have been, so low will you go.'

Then and there under the blue skies of Greece, we did some work to detach him from the black coven and also removed some black energy forms from within him. However, there was still much more that needed to be done. If Simon goes back onto drugs I suspect he will go into his own hell again. But if he keeps clear of drugs and walks the path of light which he knows so well from other lives, he could help himself and many others in this life.

Drugs are not part of the Ascension pathway. In ancient mystery schools disciples were given certain drugs in controlled circumstances to propel them to higher realms. These drugs were given to them within a framework of prayer, ritual and ceremony, which directed their spirits upwards. This was to offer them a carrot, a taste of the rewards of meditation. It was never considered to be a short cut to the Divine Light.

Indiscriminate use of drugs means the spirit can project into the astral or lower astral planes. These are the planes of the darker emotions and thought forms, in other words, hell.

Disciples of old are now reincarnating, seeking and searching again, and remembering that drugs were a short cut to Divine visions. But they only have part of the formula and very often miss the pathway or even trip into hell.

It seems that angels appear when we are ready. I had a letter from a lady who moved abroad to live with her boyfriend. Unfortunately things were not as happy as she expected, partly because his mother interfered constantly in their relationship and partly because she missed her own mother. As a result, her relationship with her boyfriend was going downhill.

One evening when he came in tired from work she gave

her boyfriend a shiatsu treatment. He fell asleep while she was standing over him. Then she saw three angels behind her guiding her where to put her hands. They said, 'Don't forget the light that you hold and who you are.'

She finished the treatment and sat on the couch, her mind buzzing. Then the angels told her that she and her mother were soulmates from the same soul group. That was why she missed her so much. From that time the emptiness of separation with her mother left, and she felt new strength and confidence which enabled her to stand up to her boyfriend's mother.

Here is the story of how a remarkable but reluctant healer received her wake up call. Veronica Blundell is one of those extraordinarily powerful healers who literally make miracles happen. She became increasingly aware of hot energy pulsing through her hands and when she touched people their problems disappeared.

At a party in Italy she talked to an old lady whose fingers were stuck backwards, so that her hands were permanently open. Operations to cut the tendons had proved useless. Veronica heard herself saying, 'Let me hold your hands.' When she let go, the old lady could open and close her hands for the first time in years.

The old lady quickly told her friend, who could not walk very well. The friend hobbled over to Veronica, who happily agreed to hold her feet. She danced for the rest of the evening.

Despite this and many other healings, Veronica still did not want to accept her powers. She had not trained as a healer. She did not understand why the healing energy flowed through her and was reluctant to accept it.

One day her fifteen-year-old son, Stephen, was in the room. He had never had a psychic experience, so when he started to get flashes in his eyes, they thought it was a migraine starting and Veronica was telling him to lie down while she pulled the curtains, when he stopped her. 'Can't you see the light?' he asked her in amazement. A shimmering light had appeared behind her shoulder and in the light glowed a radiant angel who told the boy not to be frightened and that she was his mother's angel. The angel said, 'Your mother is special. She must take up her calling as a healer. Tell her to remember who she is.' Then she held out a sceptre with an orb and said it was his mother's. Stephen said, 'The stick is solid, Mum. It's three-dimensional. Take it. You must be able to see it.' But Veronica still could not see or hear anything. However, she no longer doubted her healing abilities.

A few days later she was asked to visit a man who was dying of cancer and in terrible pain. She walked into the room and put her hands on his stomach. The pain went so abruptly that he fell asleep. The family, who had followed behind her into the room, were incredulous. 'What have you done to our Dad?' they asked.

Again Veronica heard herself say, 'He's fine. He's just reliving something which happened in his childhood that he'd forgotten about.'

When he woke the father told them of the extraordinary events from childhood he had dreamt about. From then until he passed on, he was totally free of pain while she was giving him healing.

18: DEEP CLEANSING

When we make a vow, it deeply affects our consciousness, which is why vows should never be taken lightly.
One man in his thirties told me that he had a reading
from a psychic who mentioned a marriage vow he had taken
on a beach when he was in his early teens. The psychic said
the vow was registered in his unconscious mind and was holding him back on the relationship front.

The man was absolutely amazed. He told me that he had
had a mock wedding on the beach with a girl who was a sum-
mer holiday romance when he was about fifteen. He had
thought it fun at the time and had never given it a thought
since. Now he was beginning to realise the full impact of the
mock vow and wanted it removed.

If a mock wedding in front of your friends can hold so
much power, a full wedding ceremony has even more so. So
do vows of poverty, chastity and obedience taken in other lives
during sacred ceremonies in front of many witnesses.

All past-life vows and this-life obsolete vows, such as mar-
riages which have been ended, block us from fulfilling our
potential now.

Penny was clairvoyant and psychic and had done a great
deal of self-development work. However, she still could not
understand why she was uninterested in sex. As we worked
together it became obvious that she had taken vows of chastity

as a nun and was restricted by an etheric chastity belt. During the session four chastity belts were removed from her.

I took her in meditation into a cathedral. We invoked everyone who had ever witnessed her taking a vow of chastity to enter the cathedral to witness the release of the vow. As we did this, the pews filled, mostly with nuns and monks of varying orders. She knelt in front of the priest and asked to be released from her old past-life vows which were no longer appropriate now. The priest released her with a prayer. The congregation bowed their heads.

Then four nuns took her into a side chapel, unlocked the chastity belts and took them off her. They then led her back to the front of the cathedral where she stood and pronounced herself free of that vow. As a free woman she led a procession triumphantly down the aisle.

When I saw her a few days later, she told me that her partner had treated her completely differently since that session. Up to then he had been quite distant and hands off. When she arrived home, he put his arms round her and kissed her. She knew instantly that something had shifted.

You can do similar meditations to release vows of poverty and obedience. You can even create a ceremony with some like-minded friends to let go of all your old vows.

Without realising it many people have alien implants. Beings from other galaxies are curious about humans. They do not have the opportunity to experience our reproductive system or our emotional states, so they try to monitor these with implants.

Kumeka tells us that the removal of alien implants is very important to free us to be who we truly are. While we have a foreign body within us, we cannot be pure or have total authority over our own soul.

To me it is extraordinary that such a high being should be so very caring of and interested in the small problems of people. Yet Kumeka will work with an individual to pull out deeply entrenched mental patterns. He will come to a gathering and remove alien implants. He has removed several from me.

The first time Kumeka asked me to direct a group in meditation to a place and level where he and his colleagues could remove alien implants, I was somewhat doubtful, but he later told me that 90% of implants had been removed. Several of the participants reported feeling much better.

On another occasion I was taking a weekend workshop focusing on a totally different subject. I certainly had no intention of mentioning alien implants but during lunch time I kept thinking about them. After lunch, when I asked if anyone had any questions, several hands went up together. They all wanted to know about alien implants! So I invoked Kumeka's help in releasing any that were in the participants.

The results were extraordinary. One lady wrote to me afterwards that she felt a real sense of certainty when I said Kumeka wanted to release alien implants. She said that she had not had a period for some months and her breasts had been getting harder and her stomach distended. She felt she was pregnant but all pregnancy tests showed negative results. Whenever she and her friends dowsed, however, they obtained an affirmative. The doctor said she was menopausal.

As she went into the meditative state to meet Lord Kumeka, she felt she was being lifted from her chair. She felt something being pulled out of her womb and whisked away. Next day she had a very heavy period and felt an indescribable sense of joy and freedom. She is convinced an alien baby was removed from her.

I think it unlikely that any such implant could come to fruition and be born as a human. They would usually be miscarriages.

Another lady experienced implants being removed from her stomach and uterus. After the workshop she felt impelled to make an appointment with someone who specialises in the removal of alien implants and three more were taken out of her. Presumably Kumeka can only release what people are ready to have taken out at that time.

If you feel you may have astral entities within your auric field, or alien implants, you can in meditation call on Lord Kumeka, Vywamus, Djwhal Khul and Archangel Michael to remove them for you.

Exercise —Visualisation for the release of vows

1. Relax deeply. Stroke your body with your outbreath until you feel centred and calm.

2. State your intention of releasing out-of-date vows.

3. Climb steps to a magnificent cathedral or sacred place in nature.

4. Visualise an altar with any sacred objects on it that you choose.

5. Light a candle on the altar.

6. Ask the priest or person who performed the original ceremony to appear in front of you. It does not matter if you cannot recognise or remember this person.

7. Invoke everyone who witnessed the original ceremony to enter the sacred space to witness the release of the vows.

8. Experience a releasing ceremony. Visualise whatever feels important to you.

9. Return any rings, chastity belts or other symbols of the vow.

10. Affirm your freedom in front of the assembled people.

11. Walk out of that ceremony a free person.

If you can do this in a group meditation, or create a ceremony, it is even more powerful.

Exercise — Removal of negative entities and alien implants

1. Relax.

2. Visualise yourself in a beautiful place, perhaps where there is running water or mountains.

3. When you feel deeply calm and centred, invoke Lord Kumeka, Lord of Light.

4. Invoke Vywamus, Dwjhal Kuhl and Archangel Michael.

5. When you can see or sense them near you, ask them in the name of God and All That Is Light to remove any alien implants or entities from you.

6. Sit quietly until you sense the work is complete.

7. Thank them.

8. Remember you have received grace and a blessing.

9. Close yourself down by visualising a deep blue cloak being placed over your shoulders and zipped up from your feet to your chin, the hood pulled over your head.

10. Walk out of the sacred place.

19: INTERGALACTIC WORK

Once we dedicate ourselves to the Ascension pathway we are sent out on projects. We take the light wherever we go, so we are sent where the light is needed. This may be on Earth, such as the time I thought I was going on holiday to Peru with a couple of friends of mine. Unbeknown to us we were being sent by spirit on a mission to Peru because it holds much darkness as a result of war and repression. Even more significantly Machu Picchu, which is the most important and powerful two-way interdimensional portal on the planet, has been infiltrated by the forces of darkness, allowing dark angels and aliens to enter. Our task was to dissolve some of the darkness and put light in, in order to reclaim the portal for the light.

When we returned I was told that everywhere we went we left a trail of light which had touched the hearts of everyone in the vicinity and that the earth there had absorbed the light like parched ground gratefully receiving the rain.

When you are a lightworker you carry the light wherever you go whether you do anything or not. Your presence is contributing to the raising of the vibration of the planet. In the same way wherever your thoughts go in visualisation or meditation, the light goes there. You also take the light with your spirit when you are on an out-of-body journey, such as in your dream state.

As our fourth-dimensional chakras open, we become

ready to do intergalactic work, which means that we can connect with other planets in meditation. The activation of the ninth chakra automatically means we become part of the guardianship of Earth. The activation of the tenth chakra allows us to reach into the solar system and undertake missions to other planets. When the eleventh chakra is open we become galactic beings.

During a flu epidemic I was most startled in meditation to find myself standing in front of the Council of Saturn explaining that the energy being sent to Earth was too strong, causing more shake up than humans could handle in their vibratory system, and interceding on behalf of humanity for a gentler approach.

Kumeka later told me that if only I was willing I could be used for such important missions more often. When we have dreams and meditations which involve us working with the planets and galaxies, we are doing special work.

One evening Shaaron and I were talking to Kumeka. Suddenly he stopped and told Shaaron that he wanted our help with a project.

He told us that there was a planet which was totally stuck. The planet was barren and the beings inhabiting it refused to listen or change in any way. Kumeka said that he and many of his brethren had tried to help the beings to create something different so that they could evolve but they refused to listen.

He emphasised that this piece of work was vital and urgent because the whole universe was poised in such a delicate state of balance that if even one planet was stuck, the whole system could collapse.

He wanted me to take Shaaron to the barren, rocky planet and teach the inhabitants to use the power of their creative minds to make their planet fertile and joyous.

I guided our vibrations higher and took Shaaron in meditation to this planet. Kumeka came with us but did not participate in the work. It was a fascinating project because it was clear to me that the beings who inhabited the place were terrified. We very gently sat the elders down and communicated with them. We showed them with the power of our minds what a little patch of soft green grass was like. We helped them to touch and feel it. Gradually we pictured for them flowers, trees and pools of water and encouraged them to experience these too. Then we taught them to picture, and thus manifest, the gentle mantle of nature.

We promised to return.

I told Kumeka that I felt the inhabitants had been terrified of his strong, direct approach and they needed gentle persuasion and encouragement in order to move from their paralysed state. In his noble generosity and humility he conceded that he and his colleagues so much wanted the barren planet to shift, that they had used too powerful a force in talking to them.

How incredible, I thought, that we can actually do something which helps the Ascended Masters.

Kumeka asked us to continue to visit the planet in meditation, and to take groups there too, until the inhabitants were able to understand the joy of creation and live in greenery and abundance. We did this and had the delight of sensing the planet becoming green and fertile, and the children laughing, playing and swimming. I say children; however, they are not a life-form like humans.

If you or a group you work with wish to add your energy, visit the planet in meditation and continue to teach them to create a fertile planet.

No one can offer anything open-heartedly without some return. Kumeka promised that anyone who helped to move the barren planet from its stuck state would feel the barrenness within themselves being filled.

Earth has a close link with the Pleiades and many Pleiadians have incarnated at this time. Some Star Seeds from distant galaxies step down their vibrations through the Pleiades. They are trying to get through to help us all and especially their own kind. You can ask to go to the Pleiadian light chambers for help and healing and you will receive it very powerfully.

Someone who attends one of my classes told us of an experience she had been having for some years. She would wake with her back vibrating and buzzing. At first it felt uncomfortable because it was too much. Now she was used to it. She knew it was connected to a spacecraft and that she was being energised and helped. Whenever this happened she would wake feeling full of energy and life force. It felt wonderful. She is clearly being energised for special work.

If you feel ready to undertake planetary work, sit quietly in meditation and send light to places where you sense it is needed. For intergalactic work, again sit in meditation and offer your services. Then await impressions or instructions.

20: Petitioning for Release of Karma

You do not have to bear karma longer than you want to. As a result of the Harmonic Convergence, lightworkers were released from their burden of debt. The first time I heard this I thought, 'Wonderful! I'll let it go.'

I think I expected a great weight to fall off me but of course our debt is written off only when we are ready to allow it. If we still have something to learn or if at some level we want to repay, the debt will continue and spiritual law still applies. We must ask for release.

Many of you reading this book will have repaid the backlog of debt you brought into this life, so that you are subject to instant karma. This means that any new debts you accrue must be paid back immediately and you will never be able to get away with anything ever again. Because every thought, word or action has a consequence you can accrue more karma unless you constantly witness yourself. This means that if you thoughtlessly judge someone's actions in the morning, you may find yourself in a similar situation to them in the afternoon!

It behoves us to be careful, moment by moment of what we are creating. Those angers, hurts and petty dishonesties, little jealousies and times of negativity and despair do not serve us. It is only too easy to get into debt again and the more enlightened we are the harsher the penalty.

Beliefs too have a karmic consequence. If someone comes

into incarnation with a belief they are undeserving, they will attract situations of put-down or abuse. When they respond with thoughts of anger, resentment or fear, karma is created.

I know someone who loved her cat dearly. She agonised over whether to have it put down when it was injured and finally decided to do so. The action in itself earned no karma for the intention was right. However, her feelings of guilt and doubt from that time on created karma.

Many people ask me whether there is karma attached to sex or masturbation. The answer is no. But there is often karma incurred by the visualisations and thoughts during it. Lower feelings, such as lust, guilt or neediness, pile on the debts. Loving thoughts surrounding sex can create a credit.

There has always been grace, which dissolves karma. Love is the active ingredient which activates the Law of Grace, so whenever we do something for another from pure love and compassion, we offer grace.

Illness or accident are karmic consequences of beliefs, thoughts and actions whether in this life or another. So if a child is ill, its mother, out of love and compassion, will take that child to a healer or doctor. Her act of love and the loving care of the healer or doctor is the grace which dissolves the child's karma.

If someone is drowning and a stranger dives in and rescues him, the stranger is offering grace. A therapist helping someone to see a situation differently, so that a client can find love in his heart instead of hate, is helping to activate grace.

At present many are wanting to become healers for there is a great upsurge of compassion and love in the hearts of awakened ones. Spiritual healing, Reiki healing, crystal healing and many other mental and physical therapies are becoming available now as the Divine within those with their hearts open offers grace to other human beings and to animals.

Most of us are learning lessons about relationships. Anyone who has been working on themselves will have discon- nected from parents, partners and difficult relationships and will have looked at their own inner child as well as that of the person with whom they are trying to resolve a relationship. Sometimes we do everything we can and still there seems to be a problem. There is a new dispensation to help you.

If you have tried everything to heal a relationship or situation and really done your best to understand and resolve it, you can petition God to release the debt.

I was working with a client who had done her very best over many years to heal her relationship with her mother. Finally I suggested that she ask for Divine dispensation. In meditation I took her to a higher level and she met the Lords of Karma. She told them of the inner work she had done and her great desire to heal her relationship with her mother. They consulted and then she saw one of them rubbing out a page of her akashic records, the record which is kept over lifetimes of our debits and credits. Finally she was allowed to look at the page and it was blank. She knew then that her debt had been discharged.

In my understanding there has never before in the history of our planet been such an opportunity to petition God for grace. I sense that there is a kind of Divine amnesty available now for those who are ready to take advantage of it.

Affirmations

◆ 'Divine Love and Light are flowing though me NOW releasing all limiting patterns and beliefs.'

◆ 'Divine Love flows through me whenever I think of ....'

Visualisation — To release and forgive a situation

1. Relax quietly with your eyes closed.

2. Ask that the situation you need to resolve and any person involved, appear in front of you.

3. Detach from the situation and view it from a perspective of love.

4. What can you offer to the person or situation?

5. Visualise the person receiving all they desire or the situation being resolved in a perfect way.

6. Thank the person or situation for serving you.

7. Ask for forgiveness for your part in it.

8. Open your heart to forgive anyone else.

9   Let Divine Love flow through your body and aura.

Visualisation — To petition God for release of karma
(when you feel you have tried everything)

1. Write your petition to Source

2. Close your eyes and relax.

3. Visualise yourself going up the steps to a pure white temple.

4. Cross the courtyard filled with flowers, past the beautiful fountain.

5. Ask the angels to take your petition to Source.

6. Wait to receive a reply.

7. Knock on the door of the Lords of Karma. Hand to whoever answers the reply to the petition.

8. Receive their message or response and thank them.

9. Return through the courtyard.

10. Meditate on what has happened.

21: Mantras

Saying mantras is a wonderful way to raise your light levels. Mantras are holy words or expressions which, when thought, spoken aloud or chanted, draw great light to us and build a spiritual force.

Mantras are keys to the universe. Every sound creates a pattern, which is in itself a symbol or key to unlock part of the Universal Truth. Pythagoras, who is now Lord Kuthumi, first introduced the concept of the music of the spheres, which reveals that every planet, star, plant, sea or rock in the Cosmos moves to a specific rhythm and resonates to a certain vibration. Many are repositories of ancient wisdom, which has been sealed in with mantras and mandalas.

Music, toning and mantras have specific vibrations. When we tone, play some types of music or chant certain mantras, a pattern or symbol is created. Each is a key to opening the mind and body to cosmic knowledge. So a mantra is a golden key to the Divine, facilitating access to higher awareness.

Many experiments have been carried out on the effects of different sounds on various materials, for example on metal filings and sand. As the notes were sounded the metal filings vibrated and shifted to create a shape. Now, in our scientific times, a sophisticated tonoscope is used, and the results are the same. When the final chord of Handel's *Messiah* is played through a tonoscope, it produces on a screen a perfect five-pointed star. Mantras form precise geometric patterns. The Om produces a perfect circle filled with concentric triangles.

When one tuning fork is struck, it will cause every other tuning fork in auditory range to vibrate at the same frequency. If you sound one note on a piano in a hall full of pianos, the same note will resonate on the other instruments. The brain waves of human beings in one place synchronise. Consciousness spreads.

High vibrations dissolve lower vibrations. Higher-consciousness thoughts light up lower minds. The higher consciousness therefore has the greater power and influence. Light must always win.

When we chant mantras, we are not only accessing cosmic knowledge and wisdom. We spread that wisdom to others who are ready to accept it.

The names of the Great Ones have become mantras. Avatar means the descent of Divinity into flesh. Babaji, the Yogi Christ, is a Mahavatar, which means great Avatar. He is probably one of the most beloved and well known of the Spiritual Masters, and is so powerful that he can materialise or dematerialise his body at will, often appearing to individuals or small groups of disciples. He appears as a young man of about twenty-five, with long copper-coloured hair and a radiant face and body. For many centuries, from his spiritual retreat in the Himalayas, he has been working to help human beings. He can return to the Godhead at any time but has offered himself for the redemption of humankind. He is called the Deathless Master.

Babaji has taught many of the great spiritual leaders throughout the centuries. He was the guru of Yogananda's guru and it was Babaji who sent Yogananda to America to spread Kriya Yoga, which he describes as the aeroplane method to God. The story of Babaji's rise to Ascension is told by Yogananda in the wonderful and inspiring *Autobiography of a Yogi*.

After intensive yoga practice under his guru, the renowned Siddha Yoga Master Boganathar, Babaji set out on a quest to find the great guru Agastyar. During his search in Southern

India Babaji made a solemn vow to the Divine Mother that he would remain in prayer and meditation, without moving, until Agastyar would initiate him into Kriya Yoga. For forty-eight days he sat in ceaseless devotion, through rain and baking sun, bitten by insects and emaciated. At the point of death as he repeated the name of Agastyar over and over again, the great Agastyar appeared in front of him, with food and drink. Then he initiated him into Kriya Kundalini Pranayama Yoga. He spent eighteen months in the Himalayas practising these techniques until he became a Perfect Master and entered a state of Ascension.

He is in constant communion with Christ and these two fully Illumined Masters are working together for our planet.

It has been said that you cannot speak out Babaji's name, with reverence, without calling forth a Divine blessing.

One of Sai Baba's bahjans, which are chants or hymns, consists of the name of a holy one followed by Alleluia! You can adapt it in any way you like to call in the energy of holy people, for instance, Sai Baba Alleluia! Mother Meera Alleluia! Babaji Alleluia! Yogananda Alleluia! Mother Mary Alleluia! Lord Buddha Alleluia! Mohammed Alleluia! Allah Alleluia! Lord Maitreya Alleluia! Lord Kuthumi Alleluia! Jesus Christ Alleluia! Serapis Bey Alleluia! Sanat Kumara Alleluia!

All the Ascended Masters are Lords of Light so you can prefix their names with Lord or not, according to the rhythm.

I often lie in bed at night chanting that mantra in my head and I can literally feel my body fill with light.

Or you can simply chant the name of a Great One. You can repeat this when standing in a queue, driving the car, swimming, walking or at any time that you have a free mind. Doing this is a form of meditation. When you chant the name of a Holy Master you will draw him or her to you.

For example, if you chant *Sai Baba* or *Sai Ram*, you will attract Sathya Sai Baba, the Cosmic Christ, who is incarnated at this moment in a physical body in Puttaparthi, India. (We live in incredible times!)

Hare Krishna (hail to Krishna) will draw in Lord Krishna,

Jesus Christ will bring Jesus to you. The name or mantra *Jesus Christ* has enormous power. When said meaningfully rather than automatically it draws an energy vortex of light to you.

By chanting the name of a holy person you will also draw their qualities to you. If you chant *St Francis* you will call in humility, devotion and unconditional love. *Jesus Christ* will draw unconditional love. *Gandhiji* calls forth non-violence, humility and wisdom. *Elohim, Mother Mary* or *Mother Meera* call in the Divine Mother. *St Joan of Arc* or *Archangel Michael* will bring courage.

The Divine will respond to any Divine name or form of mantra, so chanting mantras is a way of making your link to Source stronger.

Any word that you repeat becomes a mantra. People often repeat statements about lack and these become negative mantras which fill you with heaviness and darkness. Swear words are black mantras. So are constant repetitions of words such as *hate*.

Positive affirmations, especially those with rhythm and rhyme easily become mantras of light. Repeating a word such as *peace, serenity, love, calm* or *tranquillity* will bring you that energy.

Thoughts create, so when you have a mantra running through your head it is slipping into your unconscious mind and creating a good foundation for your life.

Because every mantra creates a symbol in the etheric, when enough people use a mantra, whether said silently, whispered, spoken aloud, chanted or sung, they add to one of the holy symbols or pools of Divine wisdom in the universe. When you constantly repeat a mantra, it impresses that symbol into your aura so that you can then access the Divine more easily.

People who constantly count beads on a rosary, chanting *Holy Mother of God*, will have the symbol of the Divine Mother in their personal aura. They will more easily attract that Divine Mother energy to themselves and will be adding their little bit to the power of the Divine Mother.

Om Nama Sivaya invokes Source. *Om Shanti* is a peace mantra. *Kodoish, Kodoish, Kodoish Adonai Tsbeyoth* (meaning Holy, Holy, Holy Lord God of Hosts) is one of the most powerful mantras there is.

So Ham is used by millions of people. You breathe in *So* and breathe out *Ham*. It used to be one of the most powerful of all mantras and is advocated by many pathways but Lord Kumeka told me that the planet has now moved on so it is less important than it used to be.

Needless to say if you hold a crystal while you repeat your mantras, it will be a more profound experience. You can also visualise yourself in a pyramid, and place flowers and candles around yourself.

Here are some very well known and powerful mantras:

The Great Invocation
brought through by Alice Bailey

From the point of Light within the Mind of God
Let light stream forth into the minds of men.
Let Light descend on Earth.

From the point of Love within the Heart of God
Let love stream forth into the hearts of men.
May Christ return to Earth.

From the centre where the Will of God is known
Let purpose guide the little wills of men
The purpose which the Masters know and serve.

From the centre which we call the race of men
Let the Plan of Love and Light work out
And may it seal the door where evil dwells.

Let Light and Love and Power restore the Plan on Earth.

The Lord's Prayer
used by Christians

Our Father, who art in Heaven, hallowed be Thy name.
Thy kingdom come.
Thy will be done on Earth as it is in Heaven.
Give us this day our daily bread and forgive us our trespasses as we forgive those who trespass against us.
And lead us not into temptation, but deliver us from evil. Amen.

The Mantra of the Great White Brotherhood
The Great White Brotherhood is made up of those who have mastered the physical planes and now offer themselves in service.

I am the Monad (or the soul)
I am the Light Divine
I am Love
I am Will
I am Fixed Design.

The moment I heard this one I fell in love with it, as if I recognised it from old. It calls on your mighty I AM Presence. The words *I am Fixed Design* refer to the original mission statement of your Monad. It resonates with your mission and draws you closer to it if you are not already on your monadic pathway. If you are on it, I believe it accelerates your journey.

22: Spirit Guides

Everyone has a spirit guide for no one walks on Earth alone. While our guardian angel stays with us through all our lifetimes, we attract a spirit guide according to our level of light, so we draw in new ones as we evolve.

Those who are uninterested in the spiritual life may keep the same guide throughout their life. Their guide will be more evolved than they are but will not necessarily be of the highest calibre. Stephen, who saw his mother Veronica's angel and helped to give her a wake up call, was with his mother at a station one day waiting for a friend. He started to see lights moving behind each person as they walked past. The lights were different colours and intensities but everyone had one. Then he could see that each light was a spirit guide.

As the spirit guides realised he could see them they reacted in different ways. Some did not like it and gave him a cool stare. Others came up to him and acknowledged him. Many were despondent and said of their charges, 'This one won't listen. I'll be leaving him soon and moving on. It's a waste of my energy to be with him.' If only people realised!

As we wake up from our soul sleep and start to become purer, lighter and more focused on a spiritual life, we attract higher guides to our vibrations. There are very highly evolved beings drawing close to our planet now, waiting and watching for people to raise their light frequency, so that they can make a connection. These higher guides want to channel guidance, wisdom and information through spiritual people on Earth.

Spirit guides can step down their frequency to a certain extent to meet us but we must open up and purify ourselves more in order that the highest vibration guides can connect with us. The lighter we become the more high-frequency guidance and information comes through us whether we are conscious of it or not.

Not every spirit guide has been in a physical body. If they have never incarnated on our planet, they sometimes find it hard to understand our emotions or our physical limitations. It is always up to us to take responsibility for ourselves.

Higher guides have progressed through Planes of Self-Forgiveness and are highly purified beings. They are trained for the special work of helping humans to fulfil their missions.

The more you evolve the more likely you are to have several guides helping you at any one time. They help with different aspects of your life. Someone unevolved will possibly have only one guide or helper. The lighter our frequency the more spiritual help we attract, so you may sense or be told about different guides near you. You may have a whole army of helpers in the spirit world.

Soon after my first spiritual experience in 1982 when an angel took me round the universe, I realised that I had a spirit guide but had no idea how to contact my guide or even of his or her name.

At that time, like most newly awakened people, I was eager to contact my guide or at least know the name because I was aware that the vibration of the name helps to bring the guide closer. I was given a meditation to do each night before I went to bed, in which I had to climb to the brow of a mountain, where I had to sit, ask for my guide's name and accept any impressions I was given.

That evening, full of anticipation, I sat in meditation and asked for my guide's name. A strong thought came into my head, 'Philendron'. Then suddenly a little voice piped up... 'And Nesbitt.'

'What rubbish,' I thought, really disappointed.

Every night for two weeks I sat faithfully in meditation and asked for my guide's name. Every night for two weeks I heard 'Philendron,' followed by 'And Nesbitt.' It was like a musical comedy turn and I was disgusted.

At length it was time to return to the person who had given me the meditation. She tuned in and said, 'You have two guides working with you at present. They are called Philendron and Nesbitt.'

Even now I am frequently told to accept the impressions I am given! Doubt often causes us to miss opportunities.

As I became more identified with the spiritual path and dedicated my life to walking my Truth, more guides approached me. When I started to write *Light Up Your Life*, a new guide came in to help. He impressed upon me that his name was Bartholomew. He was a wonderful, warm, gentle teacher and *Light Up Your Life* and its sequel *A Time for Transformation* were duly published. I did not talk about Bartholomew or the way he impressed me with information. Then within the space of one week I had two letters from friends saying, 'You must read the Bartholomew books which are channelled by Mary Margaret Moore. They have a wonderful energy.' A few days later, I had a phone call from someone who said she was hosting a seminar for Mary Margaret while she was in England channelling Bartholomew. Did I want to come? Without hesitation I said, 'Yes.'

I was working until the moment I left for the West Country writing up details of a new course I was planning to teach. In the car as I drove to the workshop I asked for proof that this was the same Bartholomew who was working through me. Almost as soon as Mary Margaret started channelling, she quoted word for word what I had just written. I knew that was the proof I was being offered.

I never saw Bartholomew but I did from time to time see in glimpses, in visualisations or in dreams three Native American Indian guides. Two had huge headdresses and one was young and athletic-looking with one feather and a cheeky smile.

One day I was walking in thick mist on the downs near my home. I felt totally cocooned in the white mist and very meditative. I said to the spirit world, but not aloud, 'Who are the three guides that I see? Which one is Philendron? Suddenly I saw standing in front of me a magnificent Native American Indian with a beautiful full headdress of feathers. 'Wow', I thought.

Then I said, 'Who is the young one with white moccasins and one feather?' He appeared, grinning, in front of me and said, 'I'm Red Cloud.'

So I asked, 'Well, who is the other Indian chief I sometimes see?'

Suddenly it felt as if a shaft of light came through my head and a magnificent Indian chief stood in front of me and said in a deep voice, 'I'm White Eagle.'

I gasped feeling totally unworthy and stammered, 'But I can't do any of the things they can do at White Eagle Lodge. I'm not a medium.'

He said, 'No, but you can be impressed.' Then he faded into the mist. I walked home in total shock. When I told a friend, who was a White Eagle Lodge healer, about this, she replied, 'I wouldn't tell anyone about that if I were you.' And for many years I didn't.

For many years I continued to work on my personal and spiritual development, with the aim and intention of serving the Divine.

Then one New Year's Eve, Kumeka came through to Shaaron and me. (See *Introduction to Kumeka*, p9.) He is my highest spiritual guide, an Ascended Master, and I am truly blessed to work with his energy.

23: ANGELS

Angels are surrounding us now, not only to inspire and encourage us, but also to help us and smooth our pathway to Ascension. While there have always been angels guiding and whispering to us, now there are more than ever before. They are coming to Earth at the command of God to assist with the waves of Ascension to take place.

Because of their higher-vibratory state, most people cannot see them. So they are drawing attention to their presence by floating little feathers down to us. Feathers are their calling cards.

One day I was walking along in the woods deep in thought about some problem. It was one of those rare times when I felt cut off and I could not sense or feel any help around. I stopped and said, 'Is there an angel to help me with this?' I looked down at my feet and there on the ground by my shoe was a little white feather! I knew I was being taken care of.

Soon after this a lady came to see me who was desperate to work with angels. She was very tense, and despite her great desire for the angels to help her, was filled with doubts. I have never seen anyone expressing so much doubt and hope in every sentence.

When it was time for her to relax and invite in the angels I picked up the soft blue rug in which I always wrap my clients and laid it over her. There in the middle of the blanket lay a little white feather, which had not been there earlier in the morning when I saw my first client. She was totally astounded. Needless to say, the angels arrived in force and helped her to open her heart-centre so that she could receive help for her problems.

I told these two stories at a talk one night. Everyone shared stories about feathers they had seen at unexpected times in unexpected places. Next day someone phoned me to say that after the talk she and her friends had gone to a café to eat. After their meal as they got up to leave they saw a little white feather in the middle of the table. She told me that it was a cleanly wiped table which had been completely bare when they sat down. They were thrilled that the angels had made known their presence so quickly.

At another talk a lady said that her father had been very close to the angels. He talked to them frequently. He died in a car accident and a witness to the scene told her afterwards that he thought a swan must have been hit as there were so many white feathers flying in the air! She realised now that it was the angels around him.

Angels can help us with essentially practical matters. They also have a great sense of humour.

A man who came to a workshop said, 'Thanks for your angel book. It helped me last week.' He told me he had been struggling with a stuck tap, which stubbornly refused to turn on. Just as he was deciding to give up and call a plumber, he remembered the angels. 'I wonder if there is a plumbing angel out there?' he thought. Out loud he said, 'If there is a plumbing angel, please help.'

He went back to the tap, which turned in his hand. Water flowed again.

As our vibrations rise the angels are helping to restore to us that which is ours by Divine right.

I told the story of the plumbing angel to a friend when she took me to the wonderful Hindu temple in Neasden, North London.

Thirty-three years ago, her infant son was put up for adoption. Every day since then she had prayed for him. For the last ten years, she had been searching for him through an agency.

When she arrived home after our visit to the temple, there was a letter from the agency saying the trail had gone cold. There was nothing more they could do and regretfully they must close their files. As she sat down to digest this dreadful news she thought, 'If there is a plumbing angel, there must be an angel for lost children and my son was a lost child thirty-three years ago.'

She sat quietly and asked for the angel of lost children to find her son. Seventy-two hours later, the agency phoned to say that not only had they found him but he had been searching for her and was eager to meet her. Within ten days they were reunited and she felt whole for the first time in all those years. She knew the angels had restored her son to her.

We can ask the angels to help others, being mindful at all times of our motives.

A beautifully suntanned lady told me she had just come back from holiday with her family. They had been to an isolated villa in the sun where the only entertainment was the swimming pool. Her five-year-old daughter splashed and played in the water all day, while her eight-year-old son was terrified and refused to go near it. Ten days into the holiday she started to read *A Little Light on Angels*. After a few chapters, she realised how much help angels could offer. She paused and asked an angel to help her son with his fear of the water. Later that morning her husband nudged her and whispered, 'Look!' To her amazement the boy was playing happily in the water.

Angels work with compassion through the heart.

At an *Inner Peace* workshop I explained that if we have a pain or injury in our body, our inner child is trying to give us a message which we are ignoring, and that while we deny our body's messages, we cannot experience peace.

One of the participants, whom I will call James, was an angry man. After the workshop he collared me and told me he had a back injury which was giving him considerable pain. His case was different he explained because he was injured by someone and there was a court case pending.

I commiserated before I explained that those who attacked him were external mirrors of the way he was attacking and injuring himself. This shook him but he was aware enough to understand. I reminded him he had a choice and he could either hang on to his sense of injury, his pain and his loss of inner peace or he could let go. I suggested he let go.

He did not want to hear that and went home feeling quite annoyed. As his wife was away, he had the house to himself, so he sat down in a comfy chair to think about it. He pondered until it was growing dark. Suddenly to his astonishment a light appeared in the room and an angel stood in front of him, beautiful, shining and golden. The angel showed him a movie of his life, replaying for him the horror of his childhood with a violent, alcoholic father. He was shown scenes in which as a small boy he had tried to protect his mother and been beaten. He reviewed a time when he was ten years old, with a broken leg in plaster. His drunken father had tried to beat the plaster on the leg with a stick.

As he watched the old horror, he felt the power, the warmth and the love of the angel. She said to him, 'Let go, James. Let it all go.'

Although he had not booked into the following day's *Healing with Angels* seminar, he knew he had to come and was there before me. During the course of the morning, as he told us of his experience with the angel, he started to sob. Then, for the first time ever, he shared the pain and agony of his childhood with his abusive father.

All day he could feel the angels working on him, helping him in his process of release. Thanks to them, a warm, loving, radiant man free of back pain went home after the workshop.

As we humans are raising our vibrations now and moving to higher dimensions, our etheric wings are starting to sprout from our shoulders. These are visible to some clairvoyants. Many people are feeling strange pains and tensions in their shoulders, little realising that this may be their wings growing.

By sensing your wings and focusing on them you can speed up the process of their unfoldment. It is wonderful to feel your wings. Some people's are tiny, others' enormous. Some are white, others gold, pink, rainbow, translucent. All are different.

When he connected with his wings on a workshop, one man said excitedly that this was exactly how he had felt as a child, when he could fly in his dreams and his imagination. He was remembering something of himself that he had lost. He was recognising his angelic self.

You do not have to believe in angels to access their help and guidance. Ask and they will come close to smooth your way.

As above so below. If a child loses confidence in itself, its parents' faith in the child can support it and help it to succeed. The faith of the angels in us supports us.

You do not have to believe in angels. They believe in you.

24: ARCHANGELS

Archangels are so beautiful and light that their energy is beyond our comprehension. They are enormous, their compassion infinite, their power mighty. Yet incredible as it may seem they really are working individually with humans.

Never be afraid or shy to call on them for help. Although they are mighty spiritual beings, in charge of great projects, their energy will come forth to help you if you ask for it.

Archangel Michael likes to get things done. He cuts through the stuff that holds us back, literally in one case I remember.

I had been working with a lady who told me that she had been having an affair for some time and her lover was her only source of nourishment and love. She added that her husband was a good man who loved her and that he did not know about her affair.

She had made the appointment to see me because she wanted her family life to be better, while keeping her lover! She claimed her husband did not know about her affair, so it could not affect him in any way. I reminded her that he may not be consciously aware but on an energy level, the level at which we are all connected and responding to each other, of course he knew. Almost without hesitation she agreed and added, 'In any case, he is very psychic.'

'But', she persisted, 'I won't let go of my lover. I tried once before to live without him and felt devastated. I'm not prepared to risk it again.' She was totally adamant that to cut the psychic cords with him was not an option.

She was in an entrenched position and had no intention of changing her perspective, so I guided her through a relaxation and meditation to raise her consciousness. I suggested that she look within to see if she could find another option. She closed her eyes and immediately saw herself with her husband and children. All four of them were dark but there was light shining onto her from her lover. She could see the cord which attached her to him but said the light would go out in her if she cut it.

When I suggested that we invite an angel to help, she responded eagerly that she would like to call in Archangel Michael! Immediately there was a rush of energy as the mighty Archangel entered carrying his sword. With one slash he cut the cord between her and her lover. Then he poured warmth, light and love onto her, which spread to her husband and children.

When she opened her eyes, she looked dazed and then she laughed, 'I can't believe it. I feel so different.' She left feeling absolutely clear she did not need her lover or even want to see him.

I saw her about a month later. She looked radiant and told me that she had seen the man at work and felt totally different about him. She realised he was simply a friend and since Archangel Michael had cut the cord, there was no spark between them. She told me that the consequences in her family were incredible. 'They all look so happy,' she smiled. 'My husband and I have become closer and the children have blossomed.'

We can call upon the angels and Archangels at any time. We can also ask to be taken to their retreats in the etheric, either in meditation or in our sleep time. If we do this they will work on us without our conscious participation.

Archangel Michael helps us to strengthen our Divine will and faith. He instils us with courage, strength and power and also protects us. He is often depicted with a sword in his hand.

A lady, whom I will call Liz, realised that her father, although quite old, was sexually abusing her, her children and all the female members of the family on the astral planes at night. In other words, his spirit was coming out of his body and getting sexual satisfaction from contact with the females in the family. He had been doing this for years and it was affecting them considerably, especially the little girls, for we carry what happens in our sleep time into our waking life, where it influences us unconsciously.

Needless to say, the father, in his everyday life was a pillar of society and very sexually repressed. If we deny our emotions and our sexuality, we play them out somewhere. I felt very strongly that this must be stopped; not only must the women protect themselves and their children but they must use their power to visualise him in a cage, so that he could do no more harm.

She and I visualised her old father being held in a strong cage. I was wary of any karmic consequences of doing this, so we added the proviso that this visualisation was done under grace and only if it was for the highest good.

That night one of the teenage granddaughters, who naturally knew nothing of the psychic protection we had used, had a very vivid dream. In the first part of the dream she was being freed from an oppressor. Then when she thought she was safe, suddenly a huge tiger burst from his cage. She woke up.

The father was a man of mighty willpower. His spirit, depicted by the tiger in her dream, had escaped from the strong cage into which we had placed him. From then on, before sleep, we also asked Archangel Michael to stand guard over him, so that if he tried to escape he could not harm anyone.

With others I hold a vision of creating a light centre. Those of us who hold the vision were told to organise an event for peace on 6 April 1997 which was 1000 days to the Millennium. At the end of the afternoon several hundred people formed a human star for peace and held yellow balloons as we swayed to the dance of peace.

Afterwards a very psychic lady who has attended some of my workshops approached me and said, 'Did you see the enormous golden Archangel standing in the centre of the star with its wings outstretched, embracing everyone in the star?' I did not see him but everyone felt the most extraordinary presence. Even people who were not lightworkers commented on the wonderful feeling in the star and no one wanted to move away from it.

That night I was woken by angels telling me that everyone who had stood in the star had received a blessing and our work had been done. We had sent in enough light to create a portal at that point. A portal of light is a doorway through which angels can more easily access the planet. The following night, in response to a question I had posed, I was told that Archangel Michael himself stood in the centre of the star!

Each of the Archangels has a retreat in the etheric of our planet. If you have visited one of these retreats or you feel an affinity with it, that may be an indication that you are especially linked with the Archangel who is connected to that place.

As I have already mentioned Archangel Gabriel's retreat is in the etheric above Mount Shasta, California, and you may ask to go there for purification. I talked about the etheric retreats at one workshop.

Some weeks later, one of the participants, called Margaret, told me of her experience. Before she went to sleep she asked to be taken to Archangel Gabriel's retreat. On the first night two Masters, one male and one female, came in and presented her with old memories from this and other lives, then cleared them from her aura.

On the second night she knew she must lie very still though she was not told to do so. Great energy ran through her and parts of her body where she had experienced pain in the past began to hurt. She knew it was a clearance.

On the third night she felt her colon being lifted out and two thirds of it was filled with light. Since then she has been

Archangel Retreats

Archangel	Retreat	Ray	Purpose
Michael	Banff, Canada (near Lake Louise)	Blue ray of protection (Tuesday) throat chakra	Binds evil and evil entities. Protects against attack or harm. Gives strength and courage. Strengthens Divine Will and faith.
Jophiel	South of Great Wall of China	Yellow ray of wisdom (Sunday) crown chakra	Helps people to be faithful to a belief or cause, to overcome ignorance, pride and narrow-mindedness. Call on for education and learning.
Chamuel	St Louis Missouri, USA	Pink ray of love (Monday) heart chakra	Expands the flame of love. Works with love, compassion and forgiveness. Call on him for help in letting go and transmuting old beliefs.
Gabriel	Mount Shasta, California, USA	White ray of purity (Friday) base chakra	For clarity, purity, order and discipline. He brings joy, and grace. Retreat at Findhorn for purification awakening.
Raphael	Fatima, Portugal	Green ray of balance (Wednesday) third eye	Helps travellers and healers. Brings abundance, health and healing. Stands for vision and truth.
Uriel	Tatra Mountains, Poland	Purple and gold ray of wisdom (Thursday) solar plexus	Serves peace and brings serenity, brother/sisterhood. Helps people to freedom by releasing fears and letting go of desires.
Zadkiel	Cuba	Violet ray of transmutation (Saturday) seat of the soul	Transmutes the lower energies and helps with forgiveness, diplomacy and tolerance. The Violet Flame was gained for us by St Germain to enable us to leave Earth and ascend. Zadkiel works with the Violet Flame.
Metatron	enters through Findhorn		Truth. Honesty with ourselves and others.

able to eat salads and other foods that she simply could not digest before.

Never underestimate the extent of the help available to you.

Archangel Michael's retreat is at Banff, near Lake Louise, Canada. He works with the First Ray which is blue and his day is Tuesday. You can also call on him at death to conduct you safely to your rightful place.

Archangel Metatron works mostly in another universe so his etheric retreat is not here. He enters through Findhorn, where the energy is glowing and which will become more and more of an entry portal. If you really want to work honestly on yourself, call on Archangel Metatron for help. He deals with honesty in all its forms and will help you to be honest with yourself and others. According to Kumeka the greatest blight on humankind is our ability to delude ourselves.

25: ASCENDED MASTERS

The Ascended Masters are our older brethren, highly evolved souls, also known as the Illumined Ones or the Elect. Those who have incarnated on Earth have been great teachers, prophets, leaders or creative artists. Because they have been so much more evolved than we are and have, therefore, seen life with Divine understanding they have acted and spoken differently from the average human being. As a result many of them have been martyred, ridiculed and put to death. Only subsequently have they been deified or turned into saints. They have paved the way for us and we are assured that as our turn comes to ascend we will have an easier passage.

In order to help us now many of the Ascended Masters are communicating telepathically with people whose vibrations are high enough to receive their messages. As more individuals are becoming enlightened and dedicating themselves to the spiritual path, the Illumined Ones are able to impress or channel through them great waves of light, hope, inspiration and truth. When we are ready for the responsibility which is inherent in working with the Illumined Ones they will guide and assist us in our evolution. In the past this is something that only happened to the very few who were aware and pure enough to tune in to their broadcast. Now it is available to us as soon as we raise our vibrational frequency high enough.

El Morya is working very closely with Earth to help us during this massive time of change. He belongs to the Great White Brotherhood and is the Chohan of the First Ray, which is red, and is the ray of will and power and action. Although he is from Mercury he has also had many incarnations on Earth. He was Melchior, one of the Three Wise Men; Abraham, the founder of the Jewish religion; King Solomon; and King Arthur.

El Morya works within one of the three major offices of the Spiritual Hierarchy, known as the Manu, which is headed by Allah Gobi. The other two major offices are the Office of the Christ, which is headed by Lord Maitreya, and the Office of the Mahachohan, which was headed by St Germain, who has now moved on.

There are now thousands of Ascended Masters from different cultures and various parts of the universes and some are working specifically for our planet.

A few, like *Lord Kuthumi*, have been to Earth many times on special missions. As Pythagoras, he was a philosopher who introduced the concepts of sacred geometry, higher mathematics and the music of the spheres. He was one of the Three Wise Men who followed the star to find Jesus after his birth. He reincarnated quickly as John the Beloved. During an incarnation in India as Shah Jahan he built the Taj Mahal. Possibly his best known incarnation is as St Francis of Assisi. With El Morya and Djwhal Khul, he also brought theosophy to the world.

Kuthumi is the Master or Chohan of the Second Ray, which is deep blue and embodies the qualities of love and wisdom. He is of the Brotherhood of the Golden Robe, Great Ones who take on the pain of the world. In the inner planes, in the etheric above Kashmir, Lord Kuthumi has an enormous ashram for students, as he is very involved with helping our planet to evolve now. He also has a Light Chamber in the etheric above Machu Picchu to help our understanding. His title is World Teacher. Like Jesus, the Christ, Kuthumi's teacher was Lord Maitreya, who is the Planetary Christ and head of the Spiritual Hierarchy.

Serapis Bey originated from Venus. He was a priest in Atlantis and Keeper of the White Flame. In Egypt, he was Akhenaten (Amenhotep IV). Serapis Bey was Chohan of the Fourth Ray, bringing light to humankind through the arts and he still devotes time to this. Now he has moved to the Third Ray, persuading people to use their mental processes in order to get the Will of God grounded on Earth. He also works with the Seraphim on devic and angelic evolution.

Hilarion is Chohan or Master of the Fifth ray, which is orange. He is working to bring the New Age into being. He teaches us to use our mental powers and bring forth scientific developments, by dropping the seed thoughts of scientific ideas into appropriate receptive minds. In past lives he was incarnated in Atlantis, where he worked in the Temple of Truth. In another life his guidance of the Initiates established the Oracle of Delphi in Greece. He was also Paul the Apostle. He guides anyone who is spiritually disappointed or disillusioned.

He works closely with *Master Marko* who represents the highest galactic confederation of our solar system. The capital of the solar system is on Saturn. He is also the negotiator on Earth on the Council of Saturn, so that we remain connected to our spiritual journey.

Jesus Christ, or *Sananda* as He is known in the inner planes, is the most well known and beloved of all the Illumined Ones. He is one of twelve sons/daughters of God and the only one to incarnate on our planet. According to much esoteric literature, He had past lives as Adam, Enoch, Jeshua, Joshua, Elijah and Joseph of Egypt. Norma Milanovitch in *The Light Shall Set You Free* states that He came from Venus with no karma to resolve and after His crucifixion, He reincarnated as Apollonius of Tyana, a great Master continuing to teach Divine Laws. Jesus was born as a result of immaculate conception, the spiritual thought form of God implanted non-physically into Mary, his mother. He became a high priest in the Order of Melchizedek. During the last few years of his life he was overshadowed by Lord Maitreya; in other words Lord Maitreya worked through him. Jesus passed his fourth initiation on the cross, which enabled Lord Maitreya to take his sixth initiation at the same time.

We rarely realise just how dependent the growth of the Spiritual and Angelic Hierarchy is on our growth. There have recently been great changes in the positions of those in the Spiritual Hierarchy and I hope that some of this is because we on Earth are at last coming out of the darkness, taking responsibility for our lives and raising our light vibrations. This automatically means that those who have us in charge get promoted.

Jesus is currently Chohan of the Sixth Ray, which is indigo, and the ray of devotion, religion and idealism. This ray came to Earth 2000 years ago to bring in the energy which Christ embodied. It is now moving away as it is no longer needed. In the New Age, there will be more emphasis on the Seventh Ray, claiming our power and oneness with spirit. It is said that Jesus has been ready for some time to move further on his spiritual journey but has been held back by the neediness of humankind. He has stayed because of his great love for humanity.

St Germain too has had many incarnations here to bring light to our planet. He was Samuel the prophet, Joseph of Nazareth, St Alban, Proclus the Greek philosopher, Merlin the Magician, Christopher Columbus and Francis Bacon. As Christian Rosenkreutz he founded the order of the Rosy Cross, which later became the Rosicrucians. He was the Chohan of the Seventh Ray, which is the violet ray. As a result of his intercession on our behalf he has brought to us the Violet Flame of purification which we can all access to speed our Ascension. He has recently become the Lord of Civilisation.

Mother Mary is more often known at the Virgin Mary. She protects all women and children and, because of her great compassion, is called on to intercede in healing. She was specially trained before she came into incarnation and during her life to be the mother of Jesus, the Christ. Throughout his childhood she was in touch with and guided by angels. In a past incarnation she was Isis, in Egypt, instructing Initiates in the mystery schools.

Quan Yin is the eastern counterpart of Mother Mary, working with us to balance the feminine energy on the planet.

Pallas Athena was a high priestess in Atlantis and a chief counsellor in Lemuria.

Sanat Kumara is the Planetary Logos, the boss of the universe, the greatest of the Avatars. He originated from planet Venus and has a seat in the etheric over the Gobi desert. He has never lived in a physical body on Earth but is charged with the evolution of everything and everyone on Earth, mineral, plant, animal and human. His twin flame is Lady Venus.

Vywamus is the Higher Self of Sanat Kumara. His Light, with Djwhal Khul, started the Tibetan Foundation. Part of his work with Earth is to help us dissolve all mental misconceptions and beliefs.

Djwhal Khul is often described as The Tibetan because he and Vywamus started the Tibetan Foundation. Djwhal Khul is best known for his work with Alice Bailey to bring through incredible esoteric information. He is the right-hand man of Lord Kuthumi and now teaches many of Kuthumi's students. He was one of the Three Wise Men who followed the star to find Jesus, the Christ.

Adonis is a vast Being. He was the teacher of Sanat Kumara.

Commander Ashtar, commander of the Intergalactic Fleet, belongs to the Hierarchy of the Great Central Sun.

These are some of the Ascended Masters on whom you may call for help.

26: ASCENSION CHAMBERS

In the etheric of planet Earth, in other words, in the ethers beyond the physical planet, and throughout the galaxies, there are Ascension chambers — or Light chambers — to which we can ask to go in meditation or during sleep. While we are there we will be in the energy of the Master in command. Our light quotient will be increased, our physical, mental, emotional and spiritual bodies strengthened and aligned.

By visiting these chambers in our dreams or meditations we can accelerate our rate of spiritual growth enormously.

I first came across the concept of Ascension chambers in Joshua Stone's book *The Complete Ascension Manual* and was so excited that every night I asked to visit those which appealed to me.

When I talked to Kumeka about this, he suggested that I visit Lord Kuthumi's chamber in the etheric above Machu Picchu because it is close to the Earth and therefore easier to access. It is a Light chamber to help understanding.

Lord Kuthumi also has a teaching ashram in the etheric at Kashmir for people in incarnation who truly need inspiration.

As soon as I started to ask to go to Lord Kuthumi's ashram at Machu Picchu at night, I woke in the early hours with dreams and impressions.

Kumeka told me that you have only visited the Ascension chamber and learnt or experienced what you went for if you wake with a dream.

This is an indication of a new birth within you.

Here are some snippets of what I wrote down in the night after my visits.

'Once again woke with a sense of joy and peace. Time is of equal value. No one is worth more than another.'

For many years I have held a vision of creating a spiritual ecological community. One night I was told in my dream.

'Separate yourself from those of lower consciousness and do not walk with them. Let them learn from your light. You are creating the Village Community 2000 and the motto for your community is "We Grow in Service". When we are at the fifth dimension Heaven is here on Earth with us.'

Night after night I woke with a joyous feeling and guidance, reasssurance and information about the community. This is what I wrote a few nights later:

'In my mind I was drawing the outline of a star or flower and breathing in and out down each side. This is part of the manifestation process. Lord Kuthumi was himself teaching us.'

We decided to call it the Star Centre, which will change to Star Village at a later time.

The following night at 2am I wrote:

'I woke with a central star shape buzzing and flashing brilliantly. It is the community. I am being given strength and inspiration by the Masters who already walk in the village in the Fifth dimension. I feel they are teaching symbols. Symbols will be a very important way of imparting information, so as well as posters of inspirational writings, symbols must be drawn in, particularly for the many visitors to see. Red flowers energise the activity of the symbol. Each symbolic message will have a

colour to energise it and these colours may be suggested in flowers. Creativity within the village is important. A strong team is being activated but some are reluctant to wake up.'

Two nights later I was woken with sacred geometry shapes in my head and the sounds of angels singing.

Another entry states:

'I woke and started drifting back and probably had almost done so when I was woken by a shrill whistle. They said, "You mustn't go back. It will disorientate you." I still hold a picture of the beauty of the heavens, a canopy of stars. We had a lecture on pyramids. This night work is so important I must go to bed earlier.'

One night in my dream state I was told something amazing:

'The Council of twelve running the community will together raise a light 500,000 times bigger than individual lights, and the community as a whole, one million times bigger than individuals. You are to create a new power vortex of light. You are all given keys to ascension. What we are giving you is a master key to help lots of people ascend.'

One day Kumeka told me that to travel to Lord Kuthumi's Ascension chamber in the etheric of Machu Picchu was good for raising my light quotient but it was even more important for me to travel at night for purification to Archangel Gabriel's etheric retreat. So those dreams and the information about the community stopped as I did other work.

Lord Kumeka himself has a retreat in the etheric above Caracas in Venezuela. Here he helps seekers to release limiting mental patterns, experience higher cleansing and find joy. He is incredibly powerful and it is wonderful that his energy is at last able to penetrate our dark planet.

There are two Ascension chambers in the UK, one above the rushing Findhorn river which is looked after by Archangel Gabriel, and another at Avebury.

If you have physically been to a place or wanted to go

there, it is an indication that you are connected to that Ascension seat and to the Master in charge. A few months before Kumeka suggested I might like to visit Kuthumi's seat at Machu Picchu, I had been on holiday to Peru to visit that Inca holy place.

Here are some other Ascension chambers which may appeal to you:

◈   Sanat Kumara has an Ascension chamber in Shamballa.

◈   Serapis Bey has one in Luxor.

◈   There is an Ascension seat in the Great Pyramid of Giza in the King's Chamber.

◈   There is one in Mount Shasta, California.

◈   Commander Ashtar's spaceship is an Ascension seat and there is an Ascension seat in an underground extraterrestrial craft in Africa.

     Do try to access ones connected to Earth before you try to travel to the galactic ones.

Exercise — To visit an Ascension Chamber

1.   During the day before your visit prepare yourself with pure thoughts, exercise, light eating and intention.

2.   Put paper and pen by your bed in readiness to write any impressions or information.

3.   When you go to bed hold the thought of visiting the Ascension chamber of your choice and ask to be taken there.

     You can also ask to visit an Ascension Chamber during meditation.

27: DECREES

The Universal energy is totally impersonal. It backs you one hundred per cent. If you choose to whinge and expect little, it will help you to co-create lack in your life. If you are strong, sensible, enthusiastic and expecting great things, Source will be right with you, opening doors and providing opportunities to create those great things.

As above so below. If a child asks for something from his parents thinking that they will say no, he is shooting a line. This is what many people think prayer is — asking God for something with the underlying belief and expectation that He will say no. Asking implies there is a possibility the request might be refused. That absolutely is not prayer. It is hoping or wishing.

If someone decides clearly what he wants, works out a first class proposal and presents it to his sponsor, expecting full agreement and support, he will receive all he needs to bring the plan to fruition. In the same way God responds to your energy and helps co-create your life. So prayer is telling God what you need and expecting it to be Divinely provided.

There is another aspect to prayer. While you are waiting for your prayer to be granted, you are expected to act as if it has already been granted. This is faith. Imagine you were ordering new curtains from a shop. While you wait for them to arrive, you wash the paintwork and clean the windows in preparation to put the new curtains up. You act as if the curtains will come.

The Law of Decree is similar to the Law of Prayer, but instead of putting in an order for something and waiting for it to arrive, as a Master you command. You phone the manager directly and your order is acted upon immediately. When you decree, you command the Universal energies to work on your behalf.

Another analogy to illustrate this would be: A soldier goes to his officer with a good plan and prepares everything ready for the rubber stamping. That is prayer. A commander gives orders, which only the King himself has the power to countermand. That is decree.

When we chose to incarnate on Earth, we made an agreement with the powers that be that we could take command of our lives by having the right to decree. So when you activate the Law of Decree, you set mighty forces in motion. Great Beings act on your behalf. Mountains are moved. It is a quick and powerful way to access help from the forces of light.

It is so powerful that you are warned to be careful. Only decree for something that is for your highest good and for the highest good of everyone else. When you make a decree, things will start to move in your life. After all, if mountains are to move, small hills in the way may need to be cleared out first.

I have sometimes asked if people would be willing to decree that 'Thy will be done' in their lives. The panic on some faces as they consider the possible consequences of this would be funny if it were not sad, for why are we aiming for Ascension if our will is not aligned to the Divine Will?

One woman told me that she and her mother had been in a power struggle for many lifetimes and it was time to stop it right now, no matter what. She decreed that her relationship with her mother be healed. She later wrote to me that she had twice flown right round the world to see her mother, which was certainly not intended when she made the decree. To her delight she and her mother were really close and understanding each other at last.

A man decreed that all his psychic and spiritual gifts now be returned to him. He started to open up like a flower. Part of me wanted to make a similar decree but I was wary. I checked with Kumeka who suggested this preliminary exercise before making such a decree.

Third eye cleansing exercise

1. Cup your hands and imagine them being filled with gold light.

2. Hold the cupped hands over the eyes, like an eyebath.

3. As you bathe the eyes in the golden energy affirm that all negativity in the third eye is now being released and dissolved in the light.

4. Visualise the lens of the eye being dried and polished, so that you can see clearly.

When you are ready the universe holds you and pushes you forward. On one of my workshops a woman decreed that she would use her gifts and talents in the media. Within weeks a TV company phoned her up out of the blue and asked her to present one of their programmes.

Because of its power and because we only have a part of the overall picture, it is wise to make your decree under the Law of Grace. Your intentions may be pure but on Earth we see only a small part of the whole. The Law of Grace ensures that whatever happens will be for the highest overall good and allows forces of light to override your decree if there is something better which can take place. It is your get-out clause.

For example, if you have phoned the manager directly for your order and insist on having it, you will get what you ordered. Grace ensures that if the manager is aware that something much better for you is shortly to be put onto the market, you will receive the better one even though there is a delay. Using grace, will ensure that you and everyone else gets what is best. Similarly, as the commander you may be ready to order your troops into action but the king may know that a treaty is about to be signed and another course of action would be better. So make any decrees under the Law of Grace.

You would get nowhere if you phoned the manager on his hotline whimpering that you want something. Your troops would distrust you if you gave an order, the wisdom of which you doubted yourself. Your words must be spoken with authority and command.

In accordance with spiritual law, make your decree three times.

Examples

◆   'By Divine Decree in the name of God, under the Law of Grace, I ask that................. So be it.' (Said three times)

◆   'By Divine Decree, in the name of Love and Light, under Grace, I command................. It is done.' (Said three times)

When you have made your decree, let it go completely. You do not need to repeat it. If it is for the highest overall good, the spiritual realms will bring it about and you must watch for the signs. In the meantime relax and enjoy life.

Exercise

Decree that the Divine Will be done in your life. You do not need the Law of Grace for this one!

1.   Stand in front of a friend or even better a group of people.

2.   Make sure your head is up and your shoulders back. You are commanding the universe.

3.   State aloud and with authority: 'In the name of God and all that is Light, I now Decree that Thy Will be done in my life.' Repeat twice more.

4.   Then make any other decrees you are ready for.

28: The Antakarana

Imagine continents separated by oceans. On one continent is the personality of the disciple, and on the next is the soul — or Higher Self. If the personality is uninterested in a spiritual life, it wanders about on its continent in isolation. However, when it hears the wake-up call, it is motivated to connect with the soul. Then it starts to build a bridge of spiritual practice across the ocean. It sets up a telephone link to communicate that it is coming.

The soul listens and watches to assess that the disciple is in earnest and when it really makes progress with the building of its bridge, the soul starts to build a bridge from its end, so that the two can merge.

When the soul and the personality have come together, they communicate their intention of connecting with the Monad. Then they start to build a bridge towards it. The same thing happens. As soon as they have dedicated their spiritual intent and started work on the new bridge, the Monad, or Father, lovingly builds from His end to meet them. First they meet, then they merge as one, which is Ascension.

Then, of course, the Ascended Master starts to build a bridge towards the Godhead.

So the antakarana is a rainbow bridge built between the personality, the soul and the Monad, then on to God. The bridge is built with prayer, mental discipline, visualisation, meditation and other spiritual practices. The invocation of the Mahatma energy speeds up the process.

When the disciple sets out to strengthen the thread towards the soul it is the spiritual vibration of its work which makes it thicker. First the physical, emotional, mental and spiritual bodies must be integrated. In other words, we are no longer enamoured of purely physical and material satisfaction, nor of sensory pleasures. We start to control our emotions. We use our willpower for self-discipline rather than for power struggles with others. We are interested in acquiring spiritual knowledge.

When our desire to be God-realised is more important than the temptations of life, when we can no longer be deflected or discouraged from our spiritual path by others, we are on our way and the bridge is projected towards the soul.

The soul is always connected by a cord to the pineal gland of the disciple, which is strengthened by knowledge and proper use of the mind. This cord is a mental, spiritual connection.

Just as there is always a thread from the soul to the disciple, so the silver cord connects our Monad to our heart centre. The silver cord is activated and strengthened with spiritual love energy. Psychics always talk of death taking place when the silver cord breaks and the spirit can return to the Divine Light, which is the Monad.

So at the fourth initiation, the soul merges with the personality, which is then guided by the Monad. At the fifth initiation the three rope bridges blend together to form a bridge of light and there is a meeting of soul-infused personality, Higher Self and Monad. At the sixth initiation, they integrate completely and the body turns into light. The initiate has now become an Ascended Master and can start building the bridge to God.

The antakarana is the bridge of light which allows us to move towards the Monad. It is the only way to freedom. We build the antakarana over lifetimes. At this time now there are great opportunities and much spiritual help available to enable us to complete the work and merge with our Monad. It is all speeding up.

According to Alice Bailey there are six steps needed to build
the antakarana.

1. *Intention*. You must focus on your intention to be God-realised. After all, it is the only purpose for your journey down here, so you must remain determined and dedicated to your task. All sorts of things will try to tempt you or knock you off your path but the rewards for completing the bridge are too important to let yourself be deflected. If you are building your antakarana, you are on a special mission. If you get disheartened, try, try and try again.

2. *Visualisation*. Your greatest power is your imagination. Use your imagination to focus on your bridge of light. All the visualisations in this book and other spiritual books will help you to strengthen your link to God.

3. *Projection* In order to accomplish your goal you need to use willpower. This means that, no matter what, you must picture your goal and move towards it. It helps to stay in communication with the force at the other end. So keep the telephone lines open and constantly tell them you are coming. Using the sacred mantras with focused intent and visualisation is a good way to do this.

4. *Invocation and evocation*. Constant invocation, prayer and spiritual work by the disciple evokes a response from the Monad. Remember that you are not alone. You are not doing the work alone. For every step you make towards the Monad, the Father is taking two towards you. When you seem to be crawling slowly uphill, overcoming tests and obstacles, and feel that you will never reach the end of the path, remember that the forces of light are galloping on horseback to reach you. They are on their way.

5. *Stabilisation*. At first the antakarana is as fragile as a thread. Gradually, by spiritual living and disciplines, you will weave in thread upon thread of light until the bridge is broad, strong and unbreakable.

6. *Resurrection*. As the personality moves towards the spiritual life there are three separate consciousnesses. After the merging of personality and soul, there is duality. When the soul and Monad merge, there is oneness. This is when we let go of all separation and become light. We become immortal. Constantly hold this in consciousness as you build your path of light.

As we each build our individual antakarana bridge we contribute a thread to the planetary antakarana, which connects Earth to the cosmic scheme of things.

Exercise — Visualisation

1.   Relax your whole body.

2.   Imagine a grounding cord 8″ in diameter, like a pipe, going down into the centre of the Earth. This is the foundation of your bridge.

3.   Extend the pipe, your channel, up through the chakras to the soul star above your head. See this as a great light above you.

4.   State to your soul your intention to build the antakarana bridge through spiritual work

5.   Visualise the pipe or channel extending through the chakras above you to the soul.

6.   You are now building your channel to the Monad. Call out to your Monad your spiritual aspirations, intentions and desire to serve.

7.   Picture the antakarana — a rainbow bridge of light — extended through to your Monad and to Source.

8.   Call to the Ascended Masters, the entire Spiritual Hierarchy, the angels, for help.

9.   Send mantras through the channel.

29: Ritual and Ceremony

People do not always understand the power of ritual. Yet think how difficult it is to break a simple habit. Because a habit is so deeply ingrained into the subconscious every cell in our body resists the change. Equally when we set up a positive habit — or discipline — that area of our life becomes much easier.

Ritual is a routine or habit, performed with intention and focus, which impresses both the unconscious mind and the universe. As people perform the ritual they create an energy which brings greater force to their vision.

Take the routine aspect of a ritual. If you eat your lunch at the same time at the same table each day, your body will send you hunger messages and you will find your legs walking you to that table. Your stomach will be ready and prepared to receive the food. That is the effect of routine and habit.

When you meditate in the same place and at the same time each day, it is much more effective than doing so at different times and in various places. As you sit down in your appointed way, your body and breathing will slow down and your brain waves will automatically start to go into meditation pattern.

I once asked Kumeka what would be the most helpful thing for me to do on my Ascension pathway and his response surprised me. He said, 'Get a routine.' We sometimes underestimate the importance of having a good basic routine for our spiritual work, which can then be energised with ritual.

When you start your day with a dedication ritual, you are telling the universe what you want and making it more possible. My morning ritual has changed slightly over the years as I have developed, so this is what I do now.

I stand tall and stretch up. Then I say, 'I ask my Monad to take over today with Source in overall command. I AM Light, I AM Love, I AM a pure channel for healing.' I swing my arms down and gather the Earth energy and reach up again four times. Then I ask my Monad to access the Gold Ray of Christ for my total protection three times. After that I do some yoga and meditation.

At one time I would ask to be used as a channel for light, love and healing but now I take mastery and identify with my almighty I AM Presence which is more powerful.

If you do something consistently for three weeks it becomes a routine or habit, to which ritual or even ceremony can be added.

Years ago I worked to change my deeply ingrained habit of an early morning cup of tea into a cup of hot water. For a while, no matter what, I started my day with half a cup of hot water. This turned into a full cup. Before long I did not want to drink anything except hot water in the morning. Soon after that I gave up tea and coffee completely and never missed it.

Now I have a simple ritual with my first mug of hot water. I hold it in my hands and invoke the Violet Flame of St Germain to fill the water so that every sip may purify the cells of my body. When you bless your food, it lights up and any negative energy put into it before it reached your table is transmuted. If you bless the food on the way home from the supermarket, healthfood store or wherever you shop, it will enter your home clean and pure. After all, we don't really want the handlers' energy in our food.

Kirlian photography has shown that the aura emanating from blessed food is clearer and brighter than that of unblessed food.

A simple blessing is 'I ask that this food be blessed so

that the fruits of the Earth may feed my physical body and the blessing my spiritual body.' It is always good to Om over your food.

Every salesperson knows that their attitude affects the sale. Sales patter on its own without enthusiasm or optimism is as dead as the Lord's prayer mumbled routinely and the outcome is probably similar.

Words have an energy, both the words we choose and the way they are said. This is why the words of any ritual are very important. Avoid the word 'not' and only use positive words. To make it a ceremony, use words of power like mantras and call on the greater Beings of Light.

Ritual makes an energy form. People make bedtime routines to help settle their brainwaves into sleep patterns. It is also good to set up certain nightly rituals. Prayer at night is an excellent one. First give thanks for your day and for all the blessings you have received. Then pray for others, and finally for yourself.

To use prayer in a ceremony makes it infinitely more powerful and can invoke great forces — dark or light — according to the intention.

Ritual is turned into ceremony by the use of certain music, candles, incense, holy water, movement, dance, singing, chanting, drumming, crystals. Very often specific clothing is worn.

Ceremonies usually include a specific form of words, which then have their own energy to invoke the powers. All chants, mantras and holy words enhance a ceremony.

The elements of fire, water, air and earth are used in a variety of ceremonies — for example water is used in baptisms and christenings, fire in the funeral services of many cultures, earth in burial services. (Air is represented by the talking.)

In many traditions people dance to raise enough energy to empower a ceremony.

Ritual adds power to actions. Ceremony adds power to ritual. It also harnesses group energy.

Special days have special powers. Holy Days of every culture have their own energy which makes ceremonial work done at that time infinitely more powerful. Spiritual work done at the time of the full moon has greater impact than at other times.

Meditation done in a group on a special day can move your Ascension process forward as much as three months of meditation done at other times.

When you turn a ritual into a ceremony, you call in mighty powers and do not know what forces you unleash. Make sure the intention and dedication is of the highest and purest, for ceremony is tremendously powerful.

30: ARMAGEDDON

Those of you who are reading this book will be entering or fully in the fourth dimension and will be aware that the Battle of Armageddon is taking place now. We have been told there will be seven battles between the forces of light and the forces of darkness, of which the first three will be won by the forces of darkness.

There are some very low vibrations on Earth — witness the greed and corruption, the drugs, poverty-consciousness and violence, and the energy put out by television and other media. Darkness has won the first three battles.

The last four battles must and will be won by the forces of light. The result is inevitable. The tide has already turned. The angels are flocking here and gaining entry and recognition. Enlightened old souls are amongst us and waking up. Books on personal and spiritual development are in great demand. People are going to counselling and therapy to understand and free their pain. Star Seeds are coming directly to Earth from this and other universes and taking embodiment. High-vibration people are now on Earth.

Every little bit you do to raise the light will speed the Victory.

Ninety-nine per cent of people on the planet are Earthlings, in other words, they have had all their incarnations in this third-dimensional reality and are still learning about love and light. Most have evolved through thousands of incarnations and it has been a hard pathway. They now have this incredible opportunity to free themselves from the confines of the third dimension and move through to Ascension.

The remaining one per cent are Star Seeds, who have come as visitors from other planets and galaxies to help now. Many Star Seeds have incarnated before to help in times of change but as they are visitors here most have not gone so deeply into the darkness of the planet and have relatively little karma to work out. I say 'relatively' because it is very easy to become dirty in murky waters.

For instance, as I have mentioned, Shaaron and I are from the same Monad and therefore from the same home. Although we do not originate from this universe, Shaaron has been to Earth six times and I have visited twenty-six times. We are both here to evolve, to learn in the challenging circumstances of Earth, to deal with karma and most importantly to help the planet.

All, Earthlings and Star Seeds alike, are lightworkers. All desire to return to God. Many reading this book will be Star Seeds whose purpose in incarnating now is to be a light for others. Star Seeds are consciously or unconsciously connected to the Ascended Masters. Before entering they have been assigned and agreed to their specific role; in other words, they have made etheric contracts. All Star Seeds are here to help the planet by fulfilling their pre-life agreements.

Earth is a bit like a multinational company that has a crisis. Earthlings work for the company and are expected to pull together but they have not negotiated contracts for a specific piece of work. Star Seeds are the skilled contractors and troubleshooters who are hired for specific contracts. As with all contracts the penalties for reneging on the agreements are dire and in this case there are no opt-out clauses.

In order to shake out the old density, the stuck beliefs and traumas, the Higher Beings are sending high-voltage energy surges of light to the planet. Of course, extra flows of Divine consciousness have always occurred but they used to be occasional. Now they are pulsing through the planet every six weeks or so.

These light surges, like all prana, contain symbols and codes to unlock specific memories and information within our consciousness.

Many people who think they have flu or exhaustion or some strange weakness are resisting an energy flow. If you feel unusually irritable, dizzy, fluish or unable to sleep, give yourself time and space to rest and allow the light containing new symbols to clear you out and unlock your consciousness to higher truths.

If these surges coincide with a full moon, they are, of course, more powerful.

This is what the high-voltage Divine energy charge is doing. It is bringing to the surface everything unresolved in your akashic records. Old repressed emotions, entrenched beliefs and distant past-life memories are surfacing. You may find yourself having an inexplicable desire to travel somewhere or be meeting new people who feel faintly familiar. Strange pains in your body may come up. Relax into them and sense what images surface.

It all has to be faced and resolved.

Those difficult people coming into your life may be offering you a golden opportunity to clear your akashic records, so face them with love, courage, compassion, forgiveness and understanding.

The energy surges are bringing to the surface all cellular memories that need to be cleansed and purified, going as far back as the time you were conceived. We are all very good at suppression and denial. Yet all of it has to surface — all the anger, hurt, frustration, jealousy and feelings of inferiority. Old and unexpected pains are appearing in the physical. Feelings you thought you had dealt with years ago are re-emerging to be faced at a deeper level. As they come up to the surface, move through the old ways lightly, seeing from a cosmic perspective.

If you do not face what is presented to you, it will be quickly re-presented in a way that is ten times more challenging.

A woman was sharing with me that she had a domineering, self-centred and authoritarian father. She perceived him as huge and all-powerful and had always been terrified of him. She told me he rendered her an impotent, shivering jelly. One of her life challenges was to deal with authoritarian men and she had attracted them regularly into her life. She did some personal development work to create a strong, powerful, protective father and found this very effective and helpful, so she had not attracted an angry authoritarian man into her life for some years. But now, of course, the final tests are coming.

Just when she thought she had negotiated an agreement, a phone call came out of the blue from the person she was dealing with. He had turned from a pleasant and charming man into a raging monster. She recognised the lesson galloping towards her and handled it all as calmly and clearly as she could. Time will tell whether she passed the test. If she did not, within a few months another such person will suddenly appear.

At this time there is something else we are being called on to clear. We are now called on to heal the genetic memory of our families. This is a major opportunity for individual, family and planetary resolution. It is time to purify the genetic memory which is stored in the DNA for seven generations. The sins of the fathers truly have been passed on down the generations and the time to finish it is now.

You may have incarnated with the same family again and again and be heartily sick of perpetrating the same old stuff, so any work you do will be an overall relief to your soul.

Alternatively you may have offered to enter a troubled family as a great service to them. So if your family is carrying a miasm of paralysis, insanity, abortion, violence, murder, abuse, illness (cancer, venereal diseases, TB, blindness, etc.), childhood deaths or any one of a million problems, then you have an opportunity for wonderful service and your rewards will be great. You will free past generations and future ones.

With the usual synchronicity of the universe, as I was writing this chapter, a client arrived, whom I will call Pam, a homoeopath dedicated to her healing work. She was elegant, charming and very aware but had a strong family miasm to deal with. She was suffering from a degenerative illness which resulted in creeping paralysis. She told me that her mother had suffered a stroke and become slowly more paralysed until she eventually died. This had such a heavy feel to it that I invoked the angels to help. They said her heart needed purification, so we looked to see what was blocking her heart and it was revealed she had had an abortion many years before. She did not want to have the child aborted but her powerful mother forced her into it. Her heart was full of pain and rage.

The spirit of the child had never passed over and, during the session, it came in to connect with its mother, who at last could say all the things she had wanted to say but had never been able to. Finally Pam released the child to pass over properly and it left very happily.

The angels said that her heart still was not ready for a purification and blessing. Then Pam told me that she had discovered her mother also had had an abortion. I asked that all the aborted children of the family who had not passed over come forward. Suddenly there was a huge rush as about a dozen small children came in. They were all hanging round Pam, interfering with her life. They wanted to be released and left in a shaft of light as a relative from the other side came to collect them.

Again I asked the angels to take her heart for purification but this time they showed me that the front of her heart was clear but the back was in darkness. They said a past life must be released.

Pam went quickly back into a past life where she had been a ragged peasant soldier who led a rabble into a village. There he savagely, remorselessly killed a pregnant woman with a sword and pillaged the whole village.

Afterwards he felt sick and empty as he realised it had resolved nothing. He had loved the pregnant woman but she had left him for another man, whose baby it was. Doing what he had done had created major karma.

At another level he met the spirit of the woman and child

and humbly asked for forgiveness, which eventually was granted.

This time when the angels took Pam's heart for purification and a blessing, it was granted. I saw Pam several weeks after this session. She looked radiant and reported a huge improvement in her physical state. The work she did will also have its reverberations throughout the family tree and heal past and future generations.

There is a follow-up to this story. I received a letter from Pam saying that she had just attended her first homoeopathic birth:

'I have been treating the mother all the way through her pregnancy. Her first child was induced and it was a traumatic experience she was determined not to repeat. The Mum called me on Wednesday morning to say that she was in hospital and the lack of foetal activity was causing her concern, so they were going to break the waters manually. I arrived to find her with a midwife — no doctors around — and a monitor strapped to her. I gave her remedies and the midwife was very interested and allowed me to prescribe as I wished, asking what I gave and why. The baby was born without stress after 1 hour 20 minutes' labour. My astrologer did the baby's birth chart and superimposed it on mine. Her north node of destiny is in my moon, so I was destined to be there!'

We strongly felt that this baby was the soul who could not be born because of Pam's actions in another life. So the karma had been totally redressed and more light and love added to the world.

Moment by moment we are given opportunities to side with the light.

31: ONENESS

We are all part of the Divine Oneness. God permeates every cell and atom. A stone or plant contains the same God essence as an animal, human or angel. One is indivisible. Therefore you cannot hurt a tree or a slug or another human without the reverberations touching everyone, including yourself.

Until we recognise that we are all part of the Universal consciousness and that, at an energetic level, we are in everything and everything resides within us, we cannot ascend.

Plants feel and vibrate. Would you chop a limb off a person unless it was vital to do so? Would you think of chopping an arm off someone without telling him what you were going to do? Of course not. Yet we chop branches off beautiful, living, sentient trees and bushes without warning them. Their screams of pain tear the ethers where sensitives feel and hear it. Ultimately in the same life or another the perpetrator will have that pain inflicted on him.

A sensitive was telling me how at a beauty spot near her home the local council had put up notices, telling everyone why they were felling some trees — some because they were diseased, others because they needed thinning out. A few were being cut back because they took too much light. The council did a splendid job of telling the people what was going on, *but they did not tell the trees* before they touched them, so the atmosphere in the beauty spot was filled with pain.

If someone had sent a telepathic communication to the trees about their intentions, the day before for radical work, a little while beforehand for minor work, the spirit of the tree could have prepared. If it knows what is to happen, the spirit of the tree can withdraw before it is felled or it can draw back energy from a branch which is to be lopped.

A friend of mine who was very empathetic with others and therefore picked up pain from people and the environment bought a moldavite crystal to help her live in balance and harmony with everyone without picking up their stuff. She wanted it mounted in gold and put on a chain so she could wear it round her neck. She went from jeweller to jeweller until she found one who felt right to her. The jeweller said that he would have to drill with a diamond drill through the middle of the crystal. My friend said, 'In that case please make sure you talk to it beforehand so that it knows what you are going to do.' The jeweller and his assistants were totally accepting of that. When she returned to collect it, he said to her quite seriously, 'We talked to your crystal but it wasn't very happy with us drilling a hole in it so we found another way of mounting it.' She was absolutely delighted and I am sure the crystal has served her better for all the care she took with it.

All great craftspeople love their medium. Otherwise they are merely technicians and at some level it shows, for when work is crafted with love, that Divine energy radiates from it.

The reason why Michelangelo created such wonderful statues was because he loved the marble. His love energy enabled the best to emerge from the stone.

Because all is part of the Oneness, if an animal species becomes extinct, the quality it represents leaves the planet. Dodos stood for trust and when they withdrew, trust left for us all. It then became difficult for all creatures to trust.

Every stone, crystal, plant, tree, animal, fish or person is here for a reason and is an honoured guest on the planet. At present we are abusing and torturing cows. What sort of person feeds offal to a herbivore? These beautiful and sensitive creatures are being poisoned and pushed from Earth. When a species leaves, the forces of darkness gain entry to take its place.

Animals are the younger brethren of humans, who will eventually evolve and become human. A friend of mine had a beautiful border collie. She was told that her dog was a healer and was doing soul retrieval work on her partner. When I asked Kumeka if this was true, he confirmed it and added that the dog was a Master, who would return as a human in her next incarnation.

While driving along the leafy lanes of Ireland, I was told the following story. My friend had been on a course where they were given this technique for communicating with and healing animals. They were told to visualise a healing room in which there were the perfect things they needed to help the animal. This could be an operating theatre with a surgeon, or flower remedies and aromatherapy oils or pills and potions, whatever felt right.

One of the participants had a golden retriever who was sick. One of their house rules was that the dog was not allowed on the sofa in the sitting room. The man duly visualised a healing room. The only problem was that the dog refused to enter. In the end he said to the dog, 'OK if you'll come in and let me treat you, I'll let you go on the sofa for the rest of your life.' In his visualisation the dog then came into the healing room for treatment.

At the follow-up weekend of the course, the man was bursting to tell his story. At 3.15pm, the time he did the visualisation on the previous Sunday, his wife was in the kitchen at home. To her astonishment the dog suddenly leapt from his basket and headed straight into the sitting room where he jumped onto the sofa. She spent the rest of the afternoon trying to get him off it, but he adamantly refused to budge! A bargain is a bargain at whatever level it is made.

Plants and minerals too are part of the Oneness. The densest vibration is stone. As its vibrations lighten it can experience as a plant and then as an animal.

So if you harm or merely think badly of anything outside yourself, you are damaging yourself. These are facile words to write but the reality is played out in the Law of Karma. If you harbour ill thoughts against another person or situation, you hold a ball of that low-vibration energy within you and low-vibration action will be perpetrated repeatedly against you until you release the anger and find a loving perspective.

At all times bless that ugly building, the snarling dog, the rapacious owner, that weed you are pulling out and the blessings must inevitably return to you and therefore to All.

Bless all meaningfully, not like an automaton. With compassion in your heart bless those who seem to hold you back. Bless the sick with a reassuring touch. Bless with understanding those of lower consciousness.

Oneness means that we are all mirrors of one another. Like vibrations attract like. If we do not like what we draw into our life, we are asked to look honestly in the mirror. Then we must raise our vibration. Higher vibrations must be earned by raising our consciousness but once earned and mastered we never again attract the same lower-vibration tests, circumstances or people.

The One consciousness is known as prana or chi. Within this stream of living consciousness or forcefield lie symbols. When we can access and use these symbols we have the keys to co-creation and manifestation, an inherent part of the fifth dimension and Ascension.

To access the keys and codes to creation we must be able to stay still, balanced and centred, no matter what the outside provocation. So we must be in control of our thoughts and emotions.

Serenity, balance and calm confer great power, for they enable you to be flooded with Divine energy.

We do not love an adult child more than a baby grandchild. Nor does God love an Ascended Master or a Seraph more than an animal or a lowly soul. He loves all equally.

Treating everything as Divine is a key to Ascension.

32: Codes and Keys

Consciousness streams forth from the mind of God. This contains symbols which impart truths and information to us. If our mind is jumbled or our emotions unbalanced, we either do not receive any codes or receive distorted information.

Masters have always been able to still their minds and receive high frequency truth and wisdom directly from the Mind of God.

In turn, because we are part of the Oneness and live in the forcefield of God, we too stream consciousness from our minds. This too has a vibrational frequency which in its turn manifests. Of course, low-vibration thoughts manifest low-vibration circumstances and high-vibration thoughts create high-vibrational events.

In order to ascend we must release a high-vibrational stream of consciousness all the time.

At this time, the esoteric mysteries of the universe are being unlocked. Ancient wisdom, knowledge and sacred truths, which have been buried or locked away, are being freed and released to humanity. However, it is still up to us to find and use the keys. If and when we have unlocked information which may seem beyond our comprehension, it is our task to honour it, revere it and in the stillness of our minds and hearts, open up to the vibration of truth it contains.

Very often codes are unlocked at an unconscious level. An example of this is the crop circles, formed by the angels of communication, which are keys to unlocking hidden information in the consciousness of humanity. To see a crop circle or a picture of one is to have a key turned in our mind. Many people find that when they enter a crop circle, they feel peace. Some feel anxiety. Others sense tingling or a higher vibration flows through them. Of course, there are those who do not feel or sense anything. However, the vibration within the crop circle is opening those who are ready to specific Universal information.

Some of the keys to Universal information are in ancient manuscripts now being 'found' and brought forward.

Ancient monuments like the Pyramid, the Sphinx, Stonehenge or the statues on Easter Island are coded with information. So are standing stones and certain crystals. Even old trees contain the wisdom of the universe waiting to be tapped.

Much of this knowledge, wisdom and esoteric information was sealed in with mandalas, symbols, vows and oaths, ritual and ceremony. Another thing that is happening at this time of illumination of the planet is the release of this higher knowing.

The Wise Ones of ancient times, the priests and priestesses of Atlantis, the Holy Ones of the Great Civilisations, who hold within their chakra systems the information which can decode the seals, are incarnating now in response to the trumpet call throughout the universes. Many are born enlightened. At present these are babies, children and teenagers of high-vibrational frequency who will spread the higher consciousness and ensure the Seventh Golden Age on Earth.

Some of us are torch bearers, preparing the way for them and undertaking the responsibility of parenting, grand-parenting, fostering, teaching or otherwise clearing and smoothing their paths.

Someone I know had a baby recently. She and her husband have both been lifelong vegetarians, believing only in eating organically produced food and taking only the purest of everything into their bodies. She had a reading done for the child and was told he was a Wise One, who had incarnated as a future leader. He had chosen them as his parents because his vibrations were so refined he could not take in meat or the unnatural man-made foods. Everything around him must be pure.

Jeanne Slade, who lives in Sussex, found herself moving her hands and fingers very fast while she was giving healing. She was quite unconscious of what she was doing or why. She just found it happening. I felt she could be drawing symbols very quickly. A clairvoyant watched her work with various people during these healings and was able to describe how she was doing psychic surgery, clearing inflammation and infections, realigning bones and clearing all imbalances in the body, allowing it to heal. It is very powerful work. I presume she has accessed a memory of ancient healing symbols and is automatically using them to dissolve and break down problems in her clients. Her daughter has similar powers.

It is time now for the lightworkers to wake up to their purpose. Some are reluctant to do so, which means other lightworkers must bear their burdens until they take their allotted place in the great plan.

Certain sounds are vibrational keys to wake people up. They also shatter blocks, open the heart, release emotions, heal and release information. It seems quite suddenly all over the world people are toning, chanting, playing didgeridoos, gongs, singing bowls. Each note turns part of a combination lock.

An alarm clock has been set in all lightworkers, timed to go off now. It is the persistent and unmissable wake-up call for the New Age.

We all have information encoded in our chakras, especially the higher ones. Sound helps to release this. If you stand with your forehead against a tree or an ancient stone and Om or make the sound aah, you will unconsciously wake up to more of your true divinity. Toning and chanting the Om and aah sounds in this way with a group is very powerful.

This ancient, esoteric, Divine wisdom which will raise our planet to the vibration of light will not appear in written documents suddenly found. It will emerge as higher knowing in people of the light as they decode who they are, so that a lower way of living will no longer be of interest to them. Together they will sound the higher note which wakens everyone to the fifth-dimensional vibration.

I understand that the great consciousness shift into the fifth-dimensional way of living must take place by the year 2012, which is the end of the Mayan calendar, the second coming of Christ and the midpoint of the inbreath and outbreath of Brahma. Apparently what is to happen is beyond anything we can imagine, as Divine waves sweep through the universe and lift us to the level of light. It is the most important opportunity that our souls will ever have to grow. The more prepared we are, the easier the transition and the brighter light we all become. So our personal cleansing and the cleansing of our planet must be done by then.

We have already earned the attention and help of Illumined Ones like Lord Kumeka. As we raise our light more, other Great Ones will come to help.

We are truly living in incredible times. Every single one of us who aligns to the higher vibration and dedicates themselves to help with the birthing of the planet into the fifth dimension and Ascension will receive rewards beyond their wildest comprehension.

A word of caution: A polarisation of light and dark is taking place. Do not underestimate the power of darkness which will react to the flood of light. Religious and political restriction must crumble and many souls will stumble, lost in the confusion. Do gather with other lightworkers for protection, and radiate your light even more consistently so that it shows the way for others.

Remember too that the Earth is like a great tapestry. Only the Masters have the overall plan, and each one of us who is dedicated to helping to bring this about is given our task to do. Our task is to get our work done. Do not compare yourself to others. Do not say, 'That person has more clients, earns more money, runs a hospice, does more important work, has a seat in parliament and can influence more people.' Forget all that.

As soon as you dedicate yourself to Ascension and helping the Divine Plan for the Ascension of our planet, you will be placed in the perfect slot for your talents. You will draw to you the perfect people you can guide or ignite.

You are in the perfect place at the perfect time. All is well in your world.

33: Keys to Ascension

You can ascend without knowing anything that is in this book. You can work on all these practices and still not ascend.

The reason is that to ascend we must live as a child — in our hearts. Many want to ascend but they are all logical, rational, in their heads. The head blocks the heart and for Ascension the heart must lead the head.

The child has the magical quality of innocence, which means living in our essence, being true to our feelings. The head damps down the enthusiasm, the joy and naïvety of our true selves.

To ascend we must master all aspects of our lives.

Simple guide and checklist to Ascension

The basics

1. Be yourself. Don't put on airs or graces or pretend to be who you are not.

2. Do as you would be done by.

3. See God in everything.

Physical levels

4. Clear out your house. Release clutter. Where there is physical dirt there is psychic dirt.

5. Eat as light, organic and vegetarian as possible.

6. Exercise regularly.

7. Sleep sensibly.

8. Have time for fun.

9. Set up wholesome routines and rhythms in your life.

Emotional levels

10. Look after your inner child.

11. Strengthen yourself emotionally, so that no one can upset or influence you.

12. Create cosmic wise parents to nurture, protect and encourage you.

13. Get on with your agenda and let others get on with theirs.

14. Understand others' perspectives.

15. List your enemies' good qualities.

16. Forgive readily.

17. Be open and generous-hearted.

18. Listen with your heart to understand, not your mind to respond.

Mental levels

19. Fill your mind with mantras.

20. Make daily affirmations.

21. Stay calm and centred at all times.

22. Detach from material and emotional desires.

23. Take full responsibility for your life.

24. Watch for the signals and signposts which guide your individual journey on Earth.

Choices

25. Choose your friends and associates with care.

26. Choose your thoughts, words and actions with responsibility.

27. Read and watch only those things which raise your vibrations.

28. Be moderate in all things. Master your addictions and excesses.

29. Cultivate higher qualities like kindness, generosity and caring.

Reminders

30. Accept everyone and everything as Divine. God is in the tree and the cockroach. Treat them accordingly.

31. Bless your enemies as well as your friends for they are part of the Divine Oneness.

32. Hand over your burdens to God and when you have handed them over do not grab them back.

33. Remember challenges are opportunities to grow. They would not be offered if you were not ready.

Protection

34. Ask the angels to help and protect you.

35. Protect yourself with one of the methods in this book or any other that resonates with you.

Creative visualisation

36. Remember creative visualisation is the building block of your future.

37. Visualise the barriers coming down from your heart.

38. Visualise what you want to create.

39. Visualise others receiving what they need.

Spiritual practices

40. Laugh a lot and take life lightly.

41. Meditate daily and find still quiet times for reflection.

42. Constantly give thanks and blessings.

43. Pray frequently and meaningfully. Connect with angels, guides and Ascended Masters.

44. Read spiritual books.

45. Silence is golden. If you cannot speak good, say nothing.

Service

46. Help the planet and other people.

47. Remember another person's suffering is ultimately your suffering. Hold out a helping hand.

48. Do the chores and boring jobs with good grace.

49. Sai Baba says, 'Hands that help are holier than hands that pray.'

Final check

50. Ask yourself, 'Would an Ascended Master think, say or do this?'

OTHER TITLES BY DIANA COOPER

A LITTLE LIGHT ON ANGELS

This best-selling book offers guidance on how to call on angels for help and companionship in our everyday lives, bringing the light and peace of their presence into our hearts.

Pbk 128 pages
ISBN 1 899171 51 7
£5.95 • US$10.95

GOLDEN FOOTSTEPS

Open this book at random and let the words on the page inspire and uplift you. *Golden Footsteps* is a treasure house of hope and joy.

Paperback 126 pages
ISBN 1 899171 71 7
£9.95 • US$17.95

For a complete catalogue of Findhorn Press books and products, please fill in this form and send it to:

Findhorn Press
The Park, Findhorn
Forres, Moray
Scotland IV36 0TZ
fax +44 (0)1309 690036
email books@findhorn.org

or

Findhorn Press, Inc.
P.O. Box 13939
Tallahassee
Florida 32317-3939
fax +1 850 893 3442
email info@findhornpress.com

Name _____

Address _____

_____

_____

Post Code/Zip _____